Writ

Edite

NUMBER 3 IN

**THE REPRESENTATION OF OLDER PEOPLE
IN AGEING RESEARCH SERIES**

THE CENTRE FOR POLICY ON AGEING AND
THE CENTRE FOR AGEING AND BIOGRAPHICAL
STUDIES AT THE OPEN UNIVERSITY

SERIES EDITORS
SHEILA PEACE AND JOANNA BORNAT

First published in 2004
by the Centre for Policy on Ageing
19-23 Ironmonger Row
London EC1V 3QP
Tel: +44 (0)20 7553 6500
Fax: +44 (0)20 7553 6501
Email: cpa@cpa.org.uk
Website: www.cpa.org.uk

Registered charity no 207163

British Library Cataloguing in Publication Data
A catalogue record for this book is available from the British Library

ISBN 1 901097 55 2

The Representation of Older People in Ageing Research Series is based on seminars organised by the Centre for Ageing and Biographical Studies, School of Health and Social Welfare, the Open University, and the Centre for Policy on Ageing. The papers in this volume have been revised and new material added since the seminar took place.

Titles in the series:

Biographical Interviews: the link between research and practice, edited by Joanna Bornat (No 1)

Involving Older People in Research: 'an amateur doing the work of a professional?', edited by Sheila Peace (No 2)

Everyday Living in Later Life, edited by Bill Bytheway (No 4)

Recruitment and Sampling: qualitative research with older people, edited by Caroline Holland (No 5)

*Printed in the United Kingdom by Henry Ling Limited,
at the Dorset Press, Dorchester, DT1 1HD*

CONTENTS

ACKNOWLEDGEMENTS

I would like to thank a number of people who have contributed to the production of this collection of papers. In addition to the authors, there are those who were responsible for organising the original seminar out of which this collection emerged. Gilly Crosby and colleagues at the Centre for Policy on Ageing hosted the seminar and helped to organise it, alongside colleagues at the Centre for Ageing and Biographical Studies at the Open University. The seminar was set up and chaired by Brian Gearing of the Open University and the discussant was Andrew Blaikie of the University of Aberdeen – their contributions have been invaluable in helping me put together the introductory and concluding comments to this collection. Finally, I would like to thank Angela Clark, Publicity Officer at the Centre for Policy on Ageing, without whose patience and persistence this publication would not have been possible.

Julia Johnson
Editor

1

INTRODUCTION

JULIA JOHNSON

The origin of this collection is a seminar entitled *Writing Old Age* which was held in March 1999 and jointly organised by the Centre for Ageing and Biographical Studies at the Open University and the Centre for Policy on Ageing. The three presenters were Joanna Bornat, Mike Hepworth and Hannah Zeilig and their papers, now revised, are included here together with two further papers by Jill Manthorpe and Margaret Morganroth Gullette.

Reflecting the growing interest in literary gerontology in the UK,[1] the seminar was very well attended and there was a lively discussion led by Andrew Blaikie, author of *Ageing and Popular Culture* (1999). As he pointed out in his opening comments, gerontology has been dominated by positivism, biomedicine and with the use of quasi-science to 'explain' ageing. In their disillusionment with this approach, writers such as Thomas Cole (1992) have turned to the humanities for guidance as to how we might better interpret the subjective experience of ageing as a lived process. Others such as Chris Gilleard and Paul Higgs (2000) have had problems with the manner in which gerontologists drawing on the political economy approach see structural factors as over-determining to the detriment, at times, of a closer understanding of human agency. How, Andrew Blaikie asked, can we resolve the tension between the ageing individual and the social structure, when the life course can no longer be represented as an ordered sequence of stages, but, in a late-modern or post-modern era, as a multitude of highly individualised encounters and experiences that cannot, without gross generalisation, be regarded as uniform? How, too, might we get at *meaning* – that is, what ageing feels like and the cultural freight it carries?

Such questions have led to something of a 'humanities turn' or what Gilleard and Higgs refer to as a 'cultural turn' in gerontology:

This 'cultural turn' has taken a long time to penetrate social gerontology. Stimulated to a large extent by the pioneering work of Mike Featherstone and Mike Hepworth there are signs of a growing interest in how 'ageing' is treated in everyday texts, in the media, in advertisements as well as in art. (2000, p. 3)

This collection focuses specifically on how ageing is treated in everyday texts in the form of popular fiction and auto/biography.

In 1986, Alison Lurie wrote in her novel *Foreign Affairs*, that, in classic fiction at least, almost the entire population is below age 50. Yet, as Margaret Morganroth Gullette has noted, since 1975, the year Saul Bellow published *Humboldt's Gift* and Margaret Drabble wrote *The Realms of Gold*, a series of novels have been produced in which there exist 'life affirming plots for mid- (and later-) life characters' (Gullette 1988). In stark contrast to the conventional narrative of lost innocence, pessimism and decline, Gullette sees in such literature a strong strain of meliorism – of midlife as progressive and positive and capable of improvement. Anne Tyler's recent fiction serves this purpose, for example, and likewise, up to a point, that of Anita Brookner. However, as Blaikie pointed out, there is no one goal for all, only individualised accommodations to the late twentieth and early twenty-first century malaise. Nevertheless, insofar as they involve interior dialogues, novels of ageing reflect on the process of ongoing life review.

Novels, of course, are valuable as sociological data, they possess cultural interest as purveyors of collective and subjective experience and symbolisation; they are replete with social themes, such as care provision and dealing with dementia, debates over contemporary values, expressions of prejudice; and they emphasise the importance of *diversity* in ways that social scientists, eager to construct – or deconstruct – schema, categories and discourses need reminding of. Novelists, and indeed auto-biographers, are able to write about ageing and later life as they observe and experience it, unconstrained by the disciplines of empirical research.

This collection starts with a paper by Joanna Bornat focused on the history of the poem *Kate*. In it, she addresses two fascinating questions: why has this poem been so powerful and who wrote it? The mystery of its origins means that we do not really know whether this is a piece of fiction, biography or autobiography – nevertheless, it is a form of 'writing old age'. The poem speaks particularly to those involved in the long-term care of older people and the next paper, by Jill Manthorpe, reviews novels which specifically feature residential care homes for older people. She considers ways in which such homes and those who occupy them are portrayed in popular fiction and the extent to which they mirror our ambivalence towards long-term care provision for older people in the UK. The third paper, by Hannah Zeilig, turns to the popular British fiction of the 1920s which she claims as a useful resource for learning about attitudes toward ageing in an era that, following the First World War, was explicitly dominated by a youth culture. It is an irony perhaps that many of the 1920's 'flappers', who symbolised the youth oriented culture which forms the backdrop for the novels Zeilig reviews, are the cohort of older people residing in the kind of care homes to which the novels reviewed by Jill Manthorpe refer. One of the features of Hannah Zeilig's paper is the differing ways in which the ageing of women and men were treated in early twentieth century novels. The next paper, by Mike Hepworth, reviews a selection of books by the novelist Stanley Middleton. These novels provide a more sensitive exploration of the experience of ageing from a male point of view, and Hepworth examines Middleton's use of chance encounters between the characters in them to explicate this experience. The final paper by Margaret Morganroth Gullette rounds off the collection by turning to auto/biography and the 'Conversations' between Simone de Beauvoir and Jean-Paul Sartre published in *Adieux: A Farewell to Sartre*. She addresses the question of what we can learn from these conversations regarding how we might write about our own age and ageing. She proposes a new concept of 'age autobiography' for writing the life course and writing old age.

As Andrew Blaikie said in our original seminar: 'If we begin with the question: "what constitutes an 'ageing' novel, or poem or play?" we will probably not move very far. But if we ask: "how might we better understand ageing through fiction and other forms of creative writing, and what tools for analysis does such literature furnish us with?" then we can travel a long way'. The five papers in this collection start us off along that trail.

NOTE

1. See for example Hepworth (1993; 1996; 2000) and Manthorpe (1995; 2000).

REFERENCES

Blaikie, A. (1999) *Ageing and Popular Culture*, Cambridge, Cambridge University Press.

Cole, T. R. (1992) *The Journey of Life: A Cultural History of Aging in America*, Cambridge, Cambridge University Press.

Gilleard, C. and Higgs, P. (2000) *Cultures of Ageing: self, citizen and the body,* London, Prentice Hall.

Gullette, M. M. (1988) *Safe at Last in The Middle Years*, Berkeley CA, University of California Press.

Hepworth, M. (1993) 'Old age in crime fiction', in J. Johnson and R. Slater (eds) *Ageing and Later Life*, London, Sage.

Hepworth, M. (1996) William and the old folks: notes on infantilisation, *Ageing and Society* 16(4): 423–41.

Hepworth, M. (2000) *Stories of Ageing*, Buckingham, Open University Press.

Manthorpe, J. (1995) The private residential home in fiction, *Generations Review* 5(1): 5–6.

Manthorpe, J. (2000) Dementia in contemporary fiction and biography, *Journal of Dementia Care* 9(3): 35–7.

2

FINDING 'KATE'

A poem which survives
through constant discovery

JOANNA BORNAT

We're watching a video which opens with a white caption, stark on a black background, informing us that a poem was found in the locker of an old woman who died in a geriatric hospital in Ashludie in Scotland. A few bars of music are repeated as the voice of a woman, who could be in her forties or fifties, begins to recite a poem. Now we're seeing a bare room with an unusual wooden bed on which a naked young woman lies under a white sheet. The poem continues as she moves about under the sheets, occasionally exposing parts of her body, her hands, her feet, now her naked back and shoulders. She seems to be dreaming, we see her resting her chin on her drawn up knees as she looks towards the window. She's alone with the thoughts which we imagine must be expressed through the words of the poem. We see her young body, naked from the waist up as she remembers her youth, her courtship, husband, children and then her husband's death and a lonely and fear-filled old age. The camera comes close up and frames her young face, which for a moment becomes wrinkled with age, then goes back to the young woman's face as the poem ends, with the demand: 'See me.' The question comes up on the screen, 'What do you see?' The music fades away.

These are the words of the poem we hear on the video:

> What do you see nurses
> 	what do you see?
> Are you thinking
> 	when you are looking at me
> A crabbit old woman
> 	not very wise,
> Uncertain of habit
> 	with far-away eyes,

Who dribbles her food
     and makes no reply,
When you say in a loud voice
     'do wish you'd try'.
Who seems not to notice
     the things that you do,
And forever is losing
     a stocking or shoe,
Who unresisting or not
     lets you do as you will
With bathing and feeding
     the long day to fill,
Is this what you're thinking,
     is this what you see?
Then open your eyes nurse,
     You're not looking at me.
I'll tell you who I am
     as I sit here so still,
As I use at your bidding
     as I eat at your will.
I'm a small child of ten
     with a father and mother,
Brothers and sisters who
     love one another,
A young girl of sixteen
     with wings on her feet,
Dreaming that soon now
     a lover she'll meet:
A bride soon at twenty,
     my heart gives a leap,
Remembering the vows
     that I promised to keep:
At twenty-five now
     I have young of my own
Who need me to build
     a secure happy home.

A young woman of thirty
        my young now grow fast,
Bound to each other
        with ties that should last:
At forty my young ones
        now grown will soon be gone,
But my man stays beside me
        to see I don't mourn:
At fifty once more
        babies play round my knee,
Again we know children
        my loved one and me.
Dark days are upon me,
        my husband is dead,
I look at the future
        I shudder with dread,
For my young are all busy
        rearing young of their own,
And I think of the years
        and the love I have known.
I'm an old woman now
        and nature is cruel
'Tis her jest to make
        old age look like a fool.
The body it crumbles,
        grace and vigour depart,
There now is a stone
        where I once had a heart:
But inside this old carcass
        a young girl still dwells,
And now and again
        my battered heart swells,
I remember the joys,
        I remember the pain,
And I'm loving and living
        life over again,

> I think of the years
> > all too few – gone too fast,
> And accept the stark fact
> > that nothing can last.
> So open your eyes nurses,
> > open and see,
> Not a crabbit old woman
> > look closer – see ME.

Kate, or *Crabbit Old Woman* or *Open Your Eyes*, the lines come with different titles, is a poem which has become iconic within care delivery settings, training programmes and more generally in the UK and further afield. It is one of those few poems which has developed from its apparently humble vernacular and non-literary origins to be included in the curriculum for national exams for school students, to feature in a cinema advert for a national charity and to be a typical example, 'canonised by public choice', of the nation's repertoire of memorable poems (*Guardian* 1998).

I began with a description of a video made in 1999 for the charity, Help the Aged. This short video was made by an advertising agency as a cinema advert, after the mother of one of the agency's executives gave him a copy of the poem with an account of its origins. The agency then approached the charity with the idea of an image to go with the words, which on the video are spoken by the actor Helen Mirren. The story of the making of the video, its final format and the debates which it sparked within the charity, repeat a history which I had been interested to explore for some time.

The poem on its own might be considered remarkable enough to command such special attention but what provides it with a unique quality is the story of its origins. Each time the poem is presented as being 'discovered' it is accompanied by the same account. The poem was found in the locker of a frail old woman who had been living on a hospital ward who was unable to speak but did occasionally write. After her death, sorting through her possessions the poem was found. This is the account given on first publication and, with a few variations,[1] it has remained the standard story (Searle 1973, pp. 6–9).

I am not someone who has literary training so cannot really claim to make an informed judgment about the quality of the poem's language, style and meaning. As someone working in gerontology, however, I can see how powerful the poem and the story of its origin are. It speaks for those who cannot voice their feelings. It projects a whole life behind a mask of ageing: the vigorous young woman; the mother; and then losses accompanying a decline into late life. It is full of feeling and imagery and it calls out to a younger audience, rebuking them for their lack of care, their ignorance and insensitivity. It is a biographically-based assault on ageism and, as someone who has a long-standing interest in reminiscence and oral history, I should celebrate the impact that the poem has had on professional carers and the wider public (Bornat 2001). However, I have always wondered about the story of the poem's origins and resisted its powers to seduce me into feeling guilty and unknowing.

'DISCOVERIES' OF 'KATE'

I wondered if others also were secretly ambivalent and what might be the true history of this poem. I decided to carry out a small piece of research by placing a letter in the magazine of the British Society of Gerontology, *Generations Review*, and in the Geriatric Nursing Newsletter of the Royal College of Nursing. I invited people to let me know when they first remembered reading the poem and also when they had most recently seen it published or referred to in any way.

In all I received sixteen replies, one from as far away as Brisbane in Australia.[2] Not surprisingly most of the respondents were people working in nursing contexts or who had retired from nursing. Since then, and as people have come to know that I am interested in 'sightings' of the poem, I have continued to receive copies of documents such as church magazines and training materials where *Kate* has appeared.

Amongst the responses I received two seem to me to be characteristically polarised. One was a true fan:

> *This poem is one of those 'Do you remember where you were when you heard that Kennedy had died?' experiences for me! It was late autumn 1986, I was on a one-year postgraduate CQSW* [social work qualification, JB] *student and I was reading an OU* [Open

9

University] reader about older people ... in the university library. Kate was at the front of the book. The university library is a crowded and busy place and not one where you want to be seen with tears streaming down your face, so I remember snuffling into my handkerchief and feeling pretty self-conscious! However, whenever I come across the poem, the effect is the same. I guess I could be rational and put it down to sentimentality, but I prefer to think it's because, for me, it epitomises much of the truly shameful treatment of older people in many spheres of life, not least by services supposedly designed for them and probably some guilt for my own shortcomings (at least before I was more aware of them)!

The other sent me a contrasting account of her reactions:

The first time I heard this was as a student nurse in 1977/8ish. It was given to us on a handout – photocopied from a nursing text (?). The last time was about two weeks ago [1998 JB] on an early morning Radio 4 programme – I think 'Something understood' at around 6.30am. In the intervening years it has appeared with monotonous regularity in any education/training programme for nurses related to care of older people ... Its popularity perhaps peaked at a time (late '70s and early 1980s) when there was a big emphasis on 'wrong' attitudes being at the root of all that was inadequate in hospital care of older people. I must say I got heartily sick of it and its sentimentality became increasingly cloying.

People were able to tell me about the many different contexts in which they had seen the poem over the years. One correspondent told me that she had seen *Kate* included in a GCSE poetry reader as part of her English syllabus. But apart from its contribution to their own training, people had seen it displayed in hospital wards, residential and nursing homes. As one retired officer-in-charge put it,

I honestly don't believe until you know how it 'feels' to be older and needing help you can[not] work effectively with/for the Elderly. 'Look Closer' (sic) hits you right between the eyes, and I believe it says it all. I personally gave each of my staff a copy. They in turn told me that, 'Yes, it did make a difference; it was like caring with older and wiser eyes!!'

Several people sent me a copy of *The Nurse's Reply*, a poem possibly Australian in origin.[3] Although it is written in pastiche form, mimicking the original, it has a defensive feel to it, as if the author of *Kate* had struck a raw nerve. Unpublished, it has a samizdat quality, almost a perverse subversiveness, expressing frustration and a similar lament about lack of empathy and understanding. The style and form of the poem seems to encourage creativity around the general theme of ageing and hidden youthful identity. Contrastingly, one of my correspondents included a copy of a poem written from the perspective of an older person which she said was 'taken from a church magazine'.[4]

THE POWER OF THE POEM

Gerontologists who were also educationalists had from an early stage identified the potential of *Kate* as a means to induce reflection and empathy amongst students and colleagues. After first publication the poem went on to appear in other anthologies and eventually took its place in the gerontological curriculum, making its own contribution to the development of a biographical approach to work with older people both in academic and practice settings. Gerontological education in the UK has, since its early days identified biography as a strongly enabling perspective, recognising its potential for empathy and individualised care planning (Johnson 1976; Carver and Liddiard 1978; Bornat 1989). Interestingly, some older gerontologists have begun to reflect on the biographical in their own lives, a trend initiated by Margot Jefferys, a medical sociologist by training, in a tellingly frank conference paper (Jefferys 1997).

I wanted to know more from the person who had first published *Kate* – what he thought about its literary and substantive provenance and how he had come by the poem. *Kate* first appeared in a pamphlet of poetry, titled *Elders* written by older people, published in 1973 by Chris Searle, a radical writer and teacher.[5] I interviewed him at Goldsmiths College, University of London in 1999, where he was then lecturing in educational studies.[6] Chris Searle has retained a commitment to younger people's writing and self expression and his assessment of *Kate* is that it has 'a universality and a directness which penetrated deeply into young minds' (Searle 1998, p. 44). He talked to me about the poem's achievement in terms of 'imaginative empathy' which he explains as 'using the imagination as a source of bonding and human connection'. He spoke of the poem as being enduringly powerful, a text which he has used with all sorts of groups, old, young and with children from quite diverse backgrounds: 'Pakistani, Yemeni, Caribbean children and they can all identify with it.'

Kate has powerful messages relating to gender and life meanings he argues:

> *It's a kind of 'everywoman' poem ... I remember when I read it feeling that there was an allegory within it of a person's life and the structure of a person's life, and a suggestion that she wasn't 'everywoman'. But at the same time it came back for me to the old kind of Solomon Grundy myth, you know about 'born on a Monday, married on a Thursday' – you know, the whole notion that life is a narrative, from birth to death and all the parts of living in between. It's an extraordinary poem.*

As someone who is familiar with the history of older people's long-term care one of my reservations about *Kate* has been my inability to imagine how such a poem could come to be written by someone living on a continuing care ward. Lack of privacy, personal frailty and the imposition of routines do not create opportunities for creative activity, but Chris Searle was not fazed by this:

> *I don't think we'll ever know. I mean, I accepted it as authentic. And you know it could have been that it was a concoction by a nurse, or a relative, or by somebody who was masquerading as an old person. I find that difficult to believe, because it's got the – it's stacked with life experience, which I think is one reason why it's had a kind of mythical status since then. And it's also, because of its traditional form, it's a ballad. It has all the features of a ballad: the versification of a ballad, some of the stock images, like the wings on her feet, you know I mean they're clichés, but they're also the stock images of romantic ballads. And the fact that it uses life*

itself as its structure, again is you know something that you might encounter in Africa, in various parts of the world, which gives it that kind of universality ... and the fact that it's an old woman speaking – you know, the notion of an old person reflecting, going back over their life, almost like a wise woman.

He even felt able to accept the *Nurse's Reply*, when I showed it to him, as an understandable though obvious parody:

I don't think it's an attack on the nurse. I think it's an attack on the system that doesn't give the nurse time. And that's very clear in the nurse's reply. The whole issue is that Kate is determined that she's not going to be reified. You know, she's not going to be considered a 'thing' ... she's a human being. And it's a shout for humanity. That's what gives it its enormous power. And it's the fact that Kate within the system is not being treated as a human being. And the nurse is doing her best, but the nurse herself is being forced to reify her, because of the lack of resources, the lack of time, and because the whole notion of ageing has become so systematized that the humanity is being squeezed out of it.

THE MYSTERY OF ITS ORIGINS

There seems to be no question as to the poem's literary merit, its powers to connect universally and its political messages. Does that make the question about its origins less relevant? Chris Searle had been the person who had first encountered *Kate*. He explained how this came about:

Well it goes back to 1971 when I was a teacher in the East End, in Stepney. And, together with a friend of mine who was a photographer called Ron McCormick, we produced a little book of children's poems called Stepney Words *which created a bit of a storm. I was teaching at a school in East London at the time and the authorities in the school didn't like the poems that we published, and there was a whole furore, because I was sacked, and the children came out on strike, and there was a long campaign for my reinstatement. But it created a great deal of interest around poetry – ordinary people's poetry. And in the book that we produced, that I got sacked for,*[7] Stepney Words, *there were a number of poems where the children through their imaginative empathy, imagined themselves as old people, and wrote some very stark, but very beautiful and humane poems about old age. And that created a lot of interest.*

I was also involved at that time with a group called the London Old Age Pensioners' Trade Union Committee ... it was a kind of liaison committee of different trade union representatives who were campaigning for higher pensions. This you remember was 1971, 1972. And there was a big campaign for higher pensions. There'd been a lot of agitation at the time, in that prices had risen, and people were putting it down to, you know, Wilson's devaluation and the decimalisation. And there was a feeling that the people that suffered most because of this were the old age pensioners. So, you know, there was strong indignation, and campaigns to raise the pension.

... we had a number of events. We had a poetry reading at the Half Moon Theatre in Stepney and invited a number of poets who were into their later years, but also young poets who were writing about the experience of age and trying to empathise with it and understand it. And ... out of this came this anthology called Elders. *And we really used it as a fund-raiser. And when we produced it, people kind of scoffed at the idea and laughed at the idea of poetry being used to raise funds. But it actually raised about three or four hundred quid, which was quite a lot of money in those days. We just did about two thousand copies and sold it locally. And we made a profit on it ... which we gave as a donation to the Old Age Pensions Committee to help raise the pension. And that created quite a lot of interest – you know that poetry was being used as a fundraiser.*

But the actual poetry that was being used was the poetry of the experience of elderly people. And there were some beautiful poems in the book, very stark, very moving. ... I remember we left adverts in the local press, Left press, I think some of the pensioners' organisations, that we were looking for poems. And I got a poem sent to me, this poem, Kate's poem, from a nurse. And she'd typed this poem out and she said that this was a poem by this patient of hers who was – who appeared to be a mute – didn't speak at all – but constantly asked for pen and paper. I suppose through some kind of sign, or however she asked for it. And was seen to be writing on this paper in a shaky hand ... but didn't say anything to the nurse. And the nurse obviously cared for her and looked after her.

I have quoted at length from the transcript of my interview with Chris Searle because he provides an expressive and historical account of the origins of *Kate*, enabling us to situate the poem's genesis at a particular point in political time as well as within an educational context. There are specifically English landmarks in his account but perhaps some more universally recognisable features too with his references to the emergence of a campaigning older people's movement in the 1970s and the influence of the Brazilian educationalist Paulo Freire to writing and creativity in education which draws directly on the experience of ordinary people (Freire 1972).

Chris Searle's commitment to the story of the poem's origins is convincing. However, amongst the correspondence I received, following my appeal, was a press cutting from the *Daily Mail*. Under the title, 'Poet was too shy for fame' and in answer to a reader's question about the origin of the poem, was a letter from Michael McCormack who explained:

My mother, Phyllis McCormack, wrote this poem in the early Sixties when she was a nurse at Sunnyside Hospital in Montrose.

Originally entitled Look Closer Nurse, the poem was written for a small magazine for Sunnyside only Phyllis was very shy and submitted her work anonymously.

A copy of the magazine was lent to a patient at Ashludie Hospital, Dundee, who copied it in her own handwriting and kept it in her bedside locker. When she died, the copy was found and submitted to the Sunday Post newspaper, attributed to the Ashludie patient.

Since my mother's death in 1994 her work has travelled all over the world. (Daily Mail 1998)

It seems, if this really is the end to the quest, that the answer to the mystery of its origins was there all the time. Does it matter that the origins of *Kate* are less remarkably mythic than we had thought, that indeed she was perhaps the product of a nurse's imagination? We may still need to be reminded of those silenced lives and hidden identities. Thirty years on does *Kate* speak in the same way to younger and older people? Times have changed. Those impulses which drove Phyllis McCormack to write and Chris Searle to publish may still be there but do we read the poem differently? Biographical approaches to understanding ageing are now well accepted does this therefore give the poem greater stature or perhaps make it more open to critical and more discerning analysis?

REFLECTIONS

I want to conclude by considering a number of issues both supportive to, and questioning, of *Kate*.

Perhaps the poem can be said to have continuing relevance if it enables us to evaluate critically those practices and attitudes which characterise care and support for frail older people, whether or not it was written by a nurse. Indeed, with the advent of community care policies and the closure of so many long term care hospital wards perhaps Kate's care is now everyone's responsibility, not just hospital nurses. The excellent and provoking study by Klinenberg of deaths in the Chicago heatwave of 1995, identifying the hundreds of deaths which ensued as being due to vulnerability following from the social factors of race, class and community rather than the natural causes of excessively high temperatures, suggests *Kate* is still needed for the role it can play in alerting us all to what happens when older people become invisible and excluded in some settings (2002).

However, a more critical approach might argue that the poem serves to distract us from the present person and their current needs by celebrating youthful vigour and reinforcing a view of ageing as loss and decline. More than that, does it promote a particular normative and conforming biography in its formulation of everywoman's story while denying some of those positive and informative socio-cultural understandings of ageing which more recently gerontologists have come to identify in the lives of older women, and men? For example, Tom Kitwood's emphasis on 'personhood' in care work with people with dementia draws attention to the need to identify the human qualities of each individual (Kitwood 1997), while Peter Coleman has identified the significance and content of meaning amongst frail people in very late life (Coleman *et al.* 1998). At the same time the vocabularies of embodiment (Gubrium & Holstein 1999) and well-being (Strawbridge *et al.* 2002) have become part of our repertoire of recognition of individuality in old age. And, with her rather conventionally described life stages, are we led to believe that 'Kate' in late life was without friendship (Jerrome 1993) or opportunities for sociability and socialising in institutional settings (Adams *et al.* 1998; Hubbard *et al.* 2003) or the support offered by inter-generational ties (Wenger 2001)? Her narrative offers us none of these insights and alternative experiences.

That *Kate* raises questions is confirmation that the poem still has a role to play, however often it is rediscovered, in informing and critiquing theory, policy formation and practice relating to late old age. Though we might now question some of the meanings, hidden and not so hidden, and even accept that the story of this poem's creation is a myth it does mean that those of us who spend less time with art in our daily teaching and research may have to acknowledge that, in provoking debate and emotions, a poem can affect us directly and powerfully in ways that any number of academic presentations fail to achieve.

In the end, though, for me there is more than one story about *Kate* and it is this which presents an enduring dilemma. There is the origin story, the lonely death on a hospital ward, and there is the dissemination story. *Kate* probably only gained popularity because, at the time the poem was first published it played a political role. At that time, in the early 1970s, the poem was part of a campaign which focused as much on material inequality and oppression as it did on personal and individual exclusion. Hers was the language of class as much as of difference and identity. Then her story was claimed and owned by older people themselves. Today is she more of an icon expressive of younger people's fears and guilt? We may reject the imagery invoked by *Kate* for its role in confining frail older people to the status of lost and vulnerable isolates, however, we may learn something from those who joined together to claim her as a symbol and the times which launched her on her public career.

NOTES

1. For example, Seniors Network UK, a campaigning website written by and for older people, included 'Mattie's Poem' with the story that: 'Mattie was a very dear family friend. She had been a very bright 90 year-old but her body was badly ravaged by time – she died in the Geriatric Ward of a hospital in Lanarkshire in Scotland. On one of our many visits she complained about being "spoken about" and very rarely "spoken to". She disliked being talked about as if she wasn't there! She desperately wanted to be included in the conversation. This anonymous poem reflects what Mattie experienced and felt – what many old people feel – what many disabled people feel. Seniors know this to be true – there is a young fit person inside all of us.' The poem follows with an appeal to 'Please pass on this poem to a friend – spread the message of the poem.'

    http:www.seniorsnetwork.co.uk/features/poetry/mattiespoem.htm
    [Accessed 14 April 2003]

2. I have learned while revising this article that it is also well known in Denmark. Thanks to my colleague Julia Johnson for this information.

3.   **Nurse's reply** *by Liz Hogben*

    What do we see? you ask
    What do we see?
    Yes we are thinking when we look at thee
    We may seem to be hard when we hurry and fuss,
    But there's many of you, and too few of us
    We would like far more time to sit by you and talk,
    To bathe you and feed you and help you to walk
    To hear of your lives and the things that you've done,
    Your childhood, your husband, your daughter, your son
    We grieve when we see you so sad and alone
    With nobody near you, no friends of your own
    We feel all your pain, and know of your fear
    That nobody cares though your end is so near,
    But nurses are people with feelings as well,
    And when we're together you'll oft hear tell
    Of the dear old gran in the very end bed,

And the lovely old dad, and the things that he said
We speak with compassion, and love and feel sad
When we think of your lives and the joys that you've had
When the time has arrived for you to depart
You leave us behind with an ache in our heart
When you sleep the long sleep, no more worry or care,
There are other old people, and we must be there
So please understand if we hurry and fuss –
There are many of you and too few of us.

[Although Liz Hogben has been cited as the author of this most often, Bruni Abbott, Prince Henry's Hospital, Melbourne has also been cited as the author.]

4. **Visiting the Elderly** *by Elsie Bailey*

I open my eyes – and what do I see?
      Several old ladies just like me.
      With sagging necks and wrinkled skin,
      Red-rimmed eyes and unkempt hair,
      Each frail body in a high-backed chair.
I close my eyes – and what do I see?
      The lovely girl I used to be
      With laughing eyes and flawless skin,
      Firm white teeth and golden hair
      Living each day without a care.
I open my eyes – and what do I see?
      My daughter has come to visit me.
      She is fifty now and looks so tired.
      She tells me that she cannot stay,
      She has such a lot to do today.
I close my eyes – and what do I see?
      The lovely child she used to be.
      With Joe's brown eyes and my fair hair.
      Her laughter and her winning ways
      Made the sunshine of our days.
I open my eyes – and what do I see?
      The orderly bringing the afternoon tea.
      His trolley skimming the spotless floor.
      The enamelled mugs are chipped and old

And when it reaches me the tea is cold.
I close my eyes – and what do I see?
    A table spread for afternoon tea
    With lace edged cloth and china fine.
    A silver teapot, jugs and spoons,
    Hot buttered scones and macaroons.
I open my eyes – and what do I see?
    The night nurse coming to deal with me.
    She is strong and her hands are rough.
    I dread the scolding I know I'll get
    When she discovers that I am wet.
I close my eyes – and what do I see?
    Not these rough hands which are hurting me.
    Nor this hard cot in which I'm caged.
    I place my head on Joe's warm chest
    And cradled in his arms I rest.
I open my eyes – and what do I see?
    A nurse and doctor looking at me.
    He asks her if I've settled down
    'I don't really know – it's hard to say.
    Her eyes are closed for most of the day.'

5.   Outline chronology:

1973, first published in Chris Searle (ed.) *Elders*, Reality Press, London.

1977, Gladys Elder, *The Alienated: Growing Old Today,* London, Writers and Readers Publishing Cooperative.

1978, in V. Carver and P. Liddiard (eds) *An Ageing Population*, Hodder & Stoughton with Open University Press:
'The poem was written by a woman who was unable to speak but occasionally seen to write. After she died her locker was opened and the poem was found' pp. ix–x.

1978, in *People not 'Pensioners'* published by Help the Aged Education Department, London.

1980, in Haim Hazan, *The Limbo People,* Routledge and Kegan Paul. Quotes the poem, 'Crabbit Old Woman' (sic) in full, on p. 27 as part of his ethnography of a North London Jewish Day Centre:
'The following poem which was found amongst the possessions of an old lady who had died in a geriatric hospital, and was distributed

and displayed in the Centre, provides a starting point as well as an encapsulated panorama of the whole subject...'

and n. 7 explains that the poem was:

'Printed in *News Letter*, December 1974 – a bulletin issued by the voluntary services section of the Jewish Welfare Board.'

1998, Faith Gibson, *Reminiscence and Recall: a Guide to Good Practice*, London, Age Concern, 2nd edition. 'Perhaps you already know this poem which was found in the bedside locker of an elderly woman after her death in hospital. It illustrates how important it is to look beyond present outward appearances. It also shows how much this woman wanted her various journeys or pathways through life to be understood and appreciated' (p. 14).

Title: 'A Crabbit Old Woman'.

6. I am most grateful to Chris Searle for his contribution to my research into 'Kate'.

7. See chapter 2, 'Stepney Words' in Searle (1998), for a blow-by-blow account of the events surrounding the publication of this anthology.

REFERENCES

Adams, J., Bornat, J. and Prickett, M. (1998) Discovering the present in stories about the past, in A. Brechin, J. Walmsley, J. Katz and S. Peace (eds) *Care Matters: Concepts, Practice and Research in Health and Social Care*, London, Sage.

Bornat, J. (1989) Oral history as a social movement: reminiscence and older people, *Oral History* 17(2): 16–24.

Bornat, J. (2001) Reminiscence and oral history: parallel universes or shared endeavour?, *Ageing and Society* 21(2): 219–241.

Carver, V. and Liddiard, P. (eds) (1978) *An Ageing Population: A Reader and Sourcebook*, London, Hodder & Stoughton.

Daily Mail (1998) Poet was too shy for fame, 12 March, p. 56.

Coleman, P. G., Ivani-Chalian, C. and Robinson, M. (1998) The story continues: persistence of life themes in old age, *Ageing and Society* 18(4): 389–419.

Freire, P. (1972) *The Pedagogy of the Oppressed*, London, Penguin.

Guardian (1998) Now I am old, 14 April, p. 9.

Gubrium, J. F. and Holstein, J. A. (1999) The nursing home as a discursive anchor for the ageing body, *Ageing and Society* 19(5): 519–538.

Hubbard, G., Tester, S. and Downs, M. G. (2003) Meaningful social interactions between older people in institutional care settings, *Ageing and Society* 23(1): 99–114.

Jefferys, M. (1997) Inter-generational relationships: an autobiographical perspective, in A. Jamieson, S. Harper and C. Victor (eds) *Critical Approaches to Ageing and Later Life*, Buckingham, Open University Press.

Jerrome, D. (1993) Intimacy and sexuality amongst older women, in M. Bernard and K. Meade (eds) *Women Come of Age: Perspectives on the Lives of Older Women*, London, Edward Arnold.

Johnson, M. (1976) That was your life: a biographical approach to later life, in J. M. A. Munnichs and W. J. A. van den Heuvel (eds) *Dependency and Interdependency in Old Age*, The Hague, Netherlands, Martinus Nijhoff.

Kitwood, T. (1997) *Dementia Reconsidered: The Person Comes First*, Buckingham, Open University Press.

Klinenberg, E. (2002) *Heatwave: A Social Autopsy of Disaster in Chicago*, Chicago, University of Chicago Press.

Searle, C. (ed.) (1973) *Elders*, London, Reality Press.

Searle, C. (1998) *None But Our Words*: *Critical Literacy in Classroom and Community*, Buckingham, Open University Press.

Strawbridge, W. J., Wallhagen, M. I. and Cohen, R. D. (2002) Successful aging and well being: Self-Rated compared with Rowe & Kahn, *The Gerontologist* 42(6): 727–733.

Wenger, G. C. (2001) Introduction: Intergenerational relationships in rural areas, *Ageing and Society* 21(5): 537–545.

3

AMBIVALENCE AND ACCOMMODATION
The fiction of residential care

JILL MANTHORPE

This paper takes a particular focus. It explores a series of novels where a residential care home or nursing home features in the story as a location, specific or imagined. The novels are not all set in a home; in some the home provides a backcloth to other events and locations. However, all the novels discussed permit some questioning of the role of the home and tell us something of the contemporary cultural presentation of residential care.

It is important to note that a focus on residential care does not mean that we should ignore other literary presentations of old age. Many novels discuss later life and residential care is no part of their story. Rooke (1993), for example, stresses the theme of survivorship among older people that is evident in many works of fiction. Death and illness are also not confined to later life, or institutional settings, and literary criticism (Harrison 2000) has been used to sensitise readers, often professionals, to human suffering in a variety of locations. Furthermore, other novels discuss residential care for younger adults (see Manthorpe 2003): it is not confined to the old in fiction or otherwise. The novels discussed here are widely available, recently published and, essentially, are an 'easy read'. That is not to say that they are lightweight, but they are accessible. Serious points are made but most concentrate on a good story line, with strong characterisation and a 'plot'. I have read them with enjoyment and have used them in teaching to illustrate human complexity and, with professionals, as a mirror to see how social and health care is discussed and experienced by lay audiences.

The paper starts with the theme of ambivalence, looking at family feelings and then at the ambivalent nature of consumerism in a home. It continues with an illustration of some forms of accommodation in relationships in residential care, moving to note the influence of fear as an emotion attached to residential provision. A short section looks further inside the home. The paper concludes with a broader discussion of emergent themes identified through this close reading of a selection of novels: these centre on women's perspectives, ambivalence and fear, and the cultural image of the home.

FAMILY AMBIVALENCE

The ambivalence of families to residential care is well illustrated in a popular novel *November Tree* (Stevens 1996). Helen Sullivan, who has dementia, lives in Adelaide House and is visited by her daughter Rowena. Stevens describes Rowena's feelings of 'anguish' (p. 24) when visiting her mother. Her friend Phyllida acknowledges Rowena's feelings of guilt (p. 25) but reminds her that her mother is in the best place. Rowena, too, acknowledges that the home was the 'obvious – indeed the only solution' (p. 25) and that she had been in no position to look after her mother (p. 56). Worries about the viability of residential care nonetheless trouble Rowena, who is fearful that her mother's savings will run out, that social security payments will not meet the charges, and that the alternative of a Council home is unlikely (p. 25). Adelaide House is not cheap and Rowena fears that her pension will not be sufficient to fund the fees in the future.

Stevens' outline of Rowena's ambivalence and anxiety is mirrored by her description of the physical fabric of Adelaide House. It is described as hot, stuffy, colourless, sunless, a 'characterless box'. While the care staff are not unkind, as illustrated when a nurse holds Rowena's hand as her mother lies dying, the staff reflect their environment and Rowena's ambivalence:

> The care assistant was fat, middle-aged and careworn. She looked tired and Rowena felt guilty. This weary woman, probably with a family of her own, was paid to look after her mother while she … But it was no use thinking like that. The woman probably needed the job. (p. 56)

In another view of the staff, 'a waif-like teenager' brings Rowena coffee (p. 57). Within the Home, however, a further layer of ambivalence is discernible. The residents, including Helen, appear as 'well-tended' (p. 24) as does the Home's garden. Helen is described in one visit from Rowena as being in a sitting room where the sun is trapped by the bay windows and everything outside is in a 'swirl of grey' (p. 25). The picture on the constantly on television is indistinct and flickering. In parallel with this physical impression of confusion, residents such as Helen are unable to recognise people and their consciousness is clouded:

> Helen was asleep, head thrown back on the piled pillows, toothless mouth agape, eyes deeply sunk. Her hair was wispy. She looked dead: pale and shrunken and helpless. (p. 56)

At times she does not recognise her daughters. Rowena is described as not desiring her mother's death but questioning the purpose of her mother's life, anxious about her own retirement and conscious of the accumulating expense of residential care.

Ambivalence about the care home is mirrored by presentations of the residents' old age that depict it not as a time of wisdom or dignity, but of decline. Rowena, a potentially typical spinster daughter, is not self sacrificial and rejects as impractical any expectation that she should care for her mother. But she is a loving and dutiful daughter with the ambivalence of loving her mother but not regretting her death. Stevens' sets this ambivalence in the context of a mother–daughter relationship. Rowena has long-standing resentment about her mother's befriending of Rowena's classmate. This perception of favouritism emerges in visits to Helen who at times is able to remember the friend and thus evokes Rowena's jealously.

November Tree can be used to illustrate a number of aspects of contemporary residential care. The funding, concerns about the environment, and the perceptions of relatives reflect issues with which practitioners and gerontologists are familiar. The novel conveys a sense that this is not uncommon and against this the drama of the relationship between the women, the families and friends is played out with sympathy. In my view, ambivalence provides a framework for understanding the depiction of the Home, its routines and staff, as well as the residents and Rowena's relationship with her mother.

THE AMBIVALENT CONSUMER

The privatisation of most of British residential care has created new forms of consumerism with the sector. As others have commented (e.g.

Turner and Balloch 2001), the consumer relationship is complex. Elements of this complexity are illustrated in a number of novels. This section illustrates these through discussion of the novel *The Brimstone Wedding* (Vine 1996). Its author, Barbara Vine, is a pseudonym used by the crime novelist Ruth Rendell. *The Brimstone Wedding* is set in a residential/nursing home in Suffolk; the first person narrator, Jenny, works as a care assistant. Her relationship with one resident, Stella, and the unfolding of Stella's past, form the kernel of the story. Stella is 'a lady' who has deliberated chosen Middleton Hall after a tour of East Anglia's homes. Jenny recalls that Stella said that she chose Middleton Hall as she liked her:

> It wasn't the house or the grounds or the food or the private bathroom that decided her, but me. (p. 4)

Unlike most of the other residents who are in a 'twilight world' of forgetfulness, Stella is conscious of her appearance, is elegant and lives in the present.

Jenny outlines the 'social phenomenon', the growth of private residential care, funded by the sale of people's houses. Middleton Hall is described as 'one of the best': beautiful grounds, cocktails in the evening, and views and access to the lawns. But beneath this quality are suggestions of the illness and vulnerability of the residents, and hints that the home's owner Lena is somewhat keen to encourage residents to alter their wills in her favour (p. 13) and that an uncarpeted staircase is a means to keep residents on the ground floor. Jenny reveals:

> I felt angry with Lena for not having a chair-lift. Considering what they all pay, surely she could find a few hundred for one of those. (p. 22)

It is Jenny who has to make a dental appointment for another resident and drives her to attend this on her day off (pp. 26–7). The response from the home owner is that Jenny is taking 'too much' on herself (p. 27).

Despite these undercurrents, Middleton Hall presents a well-run face, particularly to Stella's adult children, one of whom is a doctor. Stella's ability to retain the privileges of a 'paying' resident is generally respected. Care standards are high, and the infringements of her privacy are minor. Stella is dying from cancer and the care she receives at her death demonstrates that the Home is able to support dying residents. Her place is quickly filled and Jenny finds this distressing but not unexpected (p. 259). The Home is foremost a business.

The friendship between care assistant Jenny and Stella might therefore be seen as a relationship that flourishes in a slightly emotionally sterile environment. However, Stella's bequest to Jenny disturbs the status quo of the Home. Lena, the manager, accuses Jenny of being predatory:

> 'Congratulations' she said. 'Not that it took much effort, did it? Like taking a Yorkie bar from a retard, that must have been. A little kiss here, a little bit of hand-holding there, and lo and behold you're a woman of property.' (p. 263)

For Jenny the bequest is unexpected but useful and she accepts it as a gift. The patent reaction of any outsider to a sizeable bequest made by a dying woman to her carer is thus complex: sympathy is with Jenny but the relationship is open to misinterpretation of motive. Stella, as an adult, has the right to do what she likes with her money in life and to dispose of it as she wishes.

ACCOMMODATION

Residential homes in fiction become more than places, at times they provide opportunities for families to make some form of reconciliation. Their role as a place of death, rather than life, is suggested in a number of works where an older person's death provides the device for reunion or coming home.

One novel employs the dying of a mother to set the scene for a younger generation to consider the impact on them of choices made years previously. Linda Grant's novel *Still Here* (2002) sets out the traffic in death:

> Tonight someone may die, because on any night death is always possible. The company is not static, it changes all the time. It is an illusion that these are the same old people sitting in the same chairs with the same chapped legs and swollen feet. (p. 9)

The imminent death of Alix's mother provides the draw back to Liverpool and then exploration of the family's former possessions in Eastern Europe. The Home too is set in a context of former prosperity:

> ... a red sandstone monstrosity knocked up with fake turrets and crenellations, built ... by a cotton merchant around the time that the city was engorged with wealth ... (p. 7)

The scale of the Home's rooms impresses Alix on her first visit, but she sees that the 'private night world' takes over when the visitors are gone and the curtains are pulled. Then the Home tends to the physical and mental decline of its residents, to their distress, their wandering, their screaming, their smell and their deaths.

The Home has evolved out of this history of trade and empire, and specific port context of Liverpool. The novel itself takes a path down the regeneration road, with a story line of rebuilding and local politics. Within this frame, the patterns of immigration and emigration are threaded. Lotte and her family are part of the Jewish Diaspora and their generation's ageing forms the business of the Home. The staff of the Home, however, consists mainly of Irish women, recent immigrants:

> All the old Jews, every one, like their nurses and helpers ('Angels! Florence Nightingale's bog-Irish bitches, more like') had come from over the water.... The Irish girls wheel the old Jews out along the promenade at Otterspool, and the old Jews look at the river and hear the ships' sirens.... 'In your dreams' the care assistants say, for there are no more ships on the Mersey ... (p. 15)

For the Rebick family, their mother's nurse, Mary O'Dwyer, provides a calm and measured approach during their distress in the days of her dying. She provides them with coffee, suggests they go home to get rest, and talks to them about the medication. Together the Irish doctor and nurse and the Jewish family comment on their shared migration (p. 27) and their ambivalence to aspects of their homeland, religion and culture.

The first part of *Still Here* concentrates on the build-up to Alix's mother's death. The slow process of her death is finally made easier at the end by an injection of morphine. The family are against this medication initially but later agree that it is legal and best. While their mother

(Lotte) is dying, Alix and her brother have time to think about the past and their future is hinted at with first meetings and the start of a new relationship for Alix.

Within the Home, other residents who knew the family many years previously bolster their memories of their mother. 'She was a picture' recalls one elderly man (p. 15) and another woman recounts stories of their father's kindness and their mother's beauty (p. 23), although distressed to see her now as 'skin and bone'. In this way the family's own memories are confirmed and the Home again brings together shared experiences of many of its residents, despite their frailty.

FEAR OF RESIDENTIAL CARE

As shown later, some residential care is horrendous and this may colour its perceptions among older people and their relatives. A number of novels outline family members' antipathy to residential care, not so much based on fear of abuse, but on the fear of loss of person-hood (as it has become termed in policy and practice). Such relatives are not seen as finding care or responsibility particularly easy. In Bawden's novel *Family Money* (1991), the younger generation is interested in maintaining its inheritance but also voices concern about the consequences for mother (in law) of residential care:

> She's got cataracts, and funny little ways with the gentlemen, but the old girl is still <u>human</u>, not vegetable. She likes to get out and about. I couldn't bear to shove her in one of those waiting rooms for death as we did with my mother. What we've locked out horns over is where we're to live <u>with</u> her!

Family members' views vary in this story and dilemmas over risk become mixed with financial interests, but this story, like others, provides a sense of families' guilt about their decisions over residential care. Such feelings are echoed in another novel *Let's Dance* (Hegarty 1996) that sets out more explicitly the failings of community services in providing an alternative to residential care to support an older woman with increasing confusion and frailty. The authority of the critique, from a caring family doctor, underlines disappointment with care in the community. He tells the daughter, Isabel, in this novel:

'Once there's another fire, or the place gets infested, but not before, the Social Services will step in. They'll pretend they have a budget for so-called care in the community, people coming in every day for an hour, you know, but it wouldn't work. They can't afford people staying overnight. It would stagger on for a bit, and then, provided you kept your distance, they take her away. There a nice home in -------.' 'No', said Isabel. 'I couldn't consign her to that. She'd lose whatever it is she has left.' (Hegarty 1996, p. 94)

The personal touch, the knowledge of the 'person' behind the need for care, is further illustrated in a novel that has become widely known for its portrayal of caring at home, and a gendered perspective. Margaret Forster's *Have the Men Had Enough?* (1989) depicts the doubts of a daughter and grand-daughter that residential care will provide the intimate tenderness that they manage:

How can we 'put her away', as she would call it? *How can we?* (p. 125)

In this novel the differences in opinion are stated within the family, less so about the nature of residential care but more about love, duty and responsibility. Grandma's dementia is profound but variable and the work of caring for her, physical and emotional, is arduous but has its rewards for the family.

Daughter-in-law Jenny's 'ideal type' of a residential home is set against the reality of one home they visit to consider, for her the ideal would be small, intimate, bright and personal. At first, St Alma's is welcoming and attractive (p. 116), with facilities for the disabled and personal possessions. However, the home does not accept those with severe dementia and has a long waiting list. As the family's doctor reports, there are few places that will take Grandma or provide her with good care:

Recommend? No, there's none I'd actually recommend. A few I could suggest as tolerable ... (p. 138)

In the local authority home where Grandma stays briefly the fabric is poor and care seems inadequate. Grandma is given sleeping tablets and staff and fellow residents appear hostile. Her daughter- in-law removes her (p. 185):

> Hour by hour Grandma was retreating into utter dejection and I was driven mad by the evidence of her suffering. I took one look at her today, an abandoned lost heap of years, and I went and packed her case and put it in my car and then told the Matron I was taking her home. (p. 185)

INSIDE THE HOME

Fears of depersonalisation inside residential care haunt some relatives as they look from the outside in. Inside homes, some novels portray an active cast of residents with a variety of story lines, characters and genres. Bernice Rubens' (1998) *The Waiting Game* is set in a home on the south coast, The Hollyhocks: A Home for the Aged, for genteel residents, who are selected by its Matron on the basis of their social status:

> A rare aroma was class. It soft-pedalled those other effluvium that alone were offensive to the nose, and occasioned disgust and intolerable. That extra perfume of class made them bearable, and generously ascribed to simple nature. (p. 4)

Their general loathing of each other, their partnerships in crime or rivalry, or their deception about their pasts unite many residents of this Home. Matron, prejudiced and self-serving, has high expectations that her care of residents will be financially rewarded. The residents maintain their individuality, preferences and relationships outside the home. Adapting to residential life is a matter over which some exercise a degree of control:

> Mrs Feinberg ... decided she would make the best of it. She would spend less time in her room and she would mix more sociably with the other residents. (p. 78)

However, like other Homes that see themselves as superior, The Hollyhocks cannot cope with certain 'management problems' (p. 189). Mr MacPherson's deterioration and disturbance mean that Matron decides the Home would be better if this resident was settled elsewhere. Hard-hearted, manipulative Matron even feels some sympathy at Mr

MacPherson's child-like trust. Similarly disappointed, resident Mrs Harvey, who has tried three homes previously in search of a new husband, feels the loss of Mr MacPherson.

DISCUSSION

The six novels discussed here are products of the 1990s and are written for a general readership. All the authors are women, well-published and popular novelists. Fear and ambivalence, humour and seriousness, complexity and stereotype are all to be found in the novels. This discussion draws out the many possible interpretations through key themes: women's perspectives, ambivalence and fear, and the cultural image of contemporary residential care.

Women's perspectives

The novels discussed here are written by women and possibly for women. Women are the central characters in each, as the elderly residents but also as care assistants, Matrons, daughters and female kin. In general, these are middle class white women although the class divides are evident in depictions of the low status of and poor pay of the care assistants. As with many women, however, class is somewhat permeable and care assistants can be married to and thus part of the middle class, or they can move into the higher status work of professional nursing. In old age differences of class determine a person's ability to pay (or their family's means) for residential care and the quality that money appears to be able to buy. But in residential care affluence is not a guarantee of protection and the loss of mental capacity, typically through dementia, leaves older people exposed to abuse. Older women, poor or rich, may be vulnerable among strangers and their sources of help are limited.

The vulnerability of older women in residential care is illustrated in the novels, but in many ways it is feared rather than real. In particular, those who live with and care for the older person are portrayed as feeling great anxiety about the standards of residential care, and its inability to attain some of the personal or intimate aspects of their care. Women in this position, such as Bridget in *Have the Men Had Enough?* and Isabel in

Let's Dance build on a long tradition of spinster carers whose lives are committed to the care of a parent.

However, the novels reveal that current women have greater options and freedom. Alix, for instance, in *Going Home* has been living in France, and Rowena in *November Tree* is a headmistress. Neither has chosen to care full time for their mothers, and even Bridget, in *Have the Men Had Enough?* juggles her mother's caring with full-time work and an attentive boy-friend.

In residential care women are dominant as these novels reveal. They are heads of homes or owners, and are Matrons as well as health care assistants. Nurse O'Dwyer, for instance, plays a key role in the treatment decisions over Lotte in *Still Here*. Such establishments are distinct from the medical routines and hierarchies of hospitals. The novels discussed here also reveal some understanding of the neglected world of the care assistant, a largely female sphere, occupied by women but also young girls (Manthorpe in press). There is direct experience of the physical work and emotional impact of such work. Women as relatives are also not immune from financial calculations of the cost of care for their older relatives and the potential impact on their inheritance or income.

Novels at the end of the twentieth century portray many aspects of women's lives and those selected here focus on old age and the impact of frailty in old age and death. In doing so they mirror the population ageing and, as I have argued elsewhere (Manthorpe 2000), women novelists may be reflecting their own or their readers' concerns. It is no coincidence that Linda Grant has written of her mother's ageing (Grant 1998), as has Lisa Appignanesi (1999). Other commentators have noted that literary analysis has the potential 'to take us inside women's spiritual struggles, where we witness their heroic efforts to age well' (Ovrebo and Minkler 1993, p. 303). The novels discussed here are less strident but nonetheless provide a multidimensional view of women and ageing, of themselves, their families and the political economies of work and capital.

Ambivalence and fear

Fear of what lies behind the doors of residential care may result from it being unknown, undesired, and stigmatising, and many novels, not discussed here, portray older people's distress at the idea of care itself and the loss of autonomy it entails (see, for example, Rowntree 1998, p. 21). As I have noted elsewhere (Manthorpe 2002), the world of care has often been a fertile ground for plot and intense interaction. Power is, of course, easy to exercise and to excess when people are vulnerable and unable to move away or to draw on usual helping resources. A home moreover can provide a unity of place, with characters physically rooted, and not only the residents trapped.

The novels discussed here make references to fear but also to ambivalence on behalf of residents, relatives and their staff. It is not always the case that older people resent going into a Home, and the novels indicate the broad functions of current residential care in providing palliative care or accommodation for those with minor disabilities. While no one is searching for accuracy in the novel, as with soap operas the public may welcome a sense that depictions of ordinary life reflect that, albeit in an exaggerated sense at times (Gatfield with Millwood Hargrave 2003).

Davies and Nolan (2003) have recently studied carers' views of the move of a relative to a nursing home and reveal that 'making the best of it' was a common strategy for relatives who felt guilty about this. For older people, thinking about the move often began some time before it became a reality and yet for them and their carers there was little help to counter their views that this represented a failure, and scant information from professional sources. The novels discussed here confirm this temporal perspective and they help in an understanding of families where very little professional contact is evident, particularly if they pay privately for residential care. The private sector as a whole is only recently being included in research on social and health care, although novels have for some time been aware of the commercial residential care sector in its various formats (Manthorpe 1995).

Ambivalence to residential care is discernible on a number of levels. There is antipathy to institutional care, though this is not universal. There is disquiet about the financial consequences for relatives, at times portrayed as self-centred concern for their own inheritance, but also anxiety about the cost and the impact of this on families. There is a realisation that residential care is the prelude to increased frailty and death. And for women, there is perhaps particular playing out of story lines in which love, duty and guilt revolve around the mother–daughter relationship.

The cultural imagery of residential care

The novels discussed do not treat residential care in the same way. It is a location, of course, and we can see the homes depicted as presenting part of the patchwork quilt of current residential provision, with its divisions around role and function, class and ownership, care and consumption. They also present a multifaceted view of the home, from inside as a resident, or again from inside as a care assistant. From outside such homes are subject to scrutiny by relatives and from the wider community.

This variety of presentation and perception means that the image of residential care in current novels is complex. The home is familiar, part of ordinary families' experiences; people like Jenny the care assistant work in one and Rowena the headmistress visits her mother in another. It also marks the unusual, a place of death, as Grant observes 'the most violent thing of all happens here: death comes by, once or twice a week, and wrenches someone from their chair' (2002, p. 9). Atypical homes can also be the site of nefarious activities, such as financial exploitation (and in other novels, murder or major crime, see for example Staincliffe 1997). It is both in the community and outside. Such complexities are not unusual for those with an academic or professional interest in the area, that they are also conveyed in current fiction suggests that care homes constitute places where relationships are heightened at times by unconscious feelings and cultural expectations. The novels discussed here reveal that these are likely to be highly individualised.

It is easy to think of residential care as a homogeneous sector and to portray those staff inhabiting it as either 'Saints or Monsters' (Foner 1994) and residents as both helpless and hapless. It is also simplistic to see relatives as having total agency, or none at all. The novels discussed here present residential care in its complexity and I would argue that vigilance to cultural representations of services, professions and policy is fruitful: deserving further thought, analysis and discussion.

REFERENCES

Appignanesi, L. (1999) *Losing the Dead*, London, Chatto and Windus.

Bawden, N. (1991) *Family Money*, London, Virago.

Davies, S. and Nolan, M. (2003) 'Making the best of things': relatives' experiences of decisions about care-home entry, *Ageing & Society* 23(4): 429–450.

Foner, N. (1994) Nursing home aides: saints or monsters?, *The Gerontologist* 34(2): 245–250.

Forster, M. (1989) *Have the Men Had Enough?*, Harmondsworth, Penguin.

Gatfield, L. with Millwood Hargrave, A. (2003) *Dramatic Licence: Fact or Fiction?*, London, Broadcasting Standards Commission.

Grant, L. (1998) *Remind Me Who I Am, Again*, London, Granta.

Grant, L. (2002) *Still Here*, London, Little, Brown.

Harrison, E. (2000) Intolerable human suffering and the role of the ancestor: literary criticism as a means of analysis, *Journal of Advanced Nursing* 32(3): 689–694.

Hegarty, F. (1996) *Let's Dance*, Harmondsworth, Penguin.

Manthorpe, J. (1995) Private residential care in fiction, *Generations Review* 5(1): 6.

Manthorpe, J. (2000) Dementia in contemporary fiction and biography, *Journal of Dementia Care* (May): 35–37.

Manthorpe, J. (2002) Holding a mirror up to the world, *Journal of Dementia Care* (March): 29–31.

Manthorpe, J. (2003) Literature reviewed: fiction, learning disability and the professional perspective, *Journal of Social Work* 3(3).

Manthorpe, J. (in press) A child's eye view: dementia in children's literature, *British Journal of Social Work*.

Ovrebo, B. and Minkler, M. (1993) The lives of older women: perspectives from political economy and the humanities, in T. R. Cole (ed.) *Voices and Visions of Aging*, New York, Springer, pp. 289–308.

Rooke, C. (1993) Old age in contemporary fiction: a new paradigm of hope, in T. R. Cole, D. Van Tassel and R. Kastenbaum (eds) *Handbook of the Humanities and Aging*, New York, Springer, pp. 241–257.

Rowntree, K. (1998) *Mr Brightly's Evening Off*, London, Black Swan.

Rubens, B. (1998) *The Waiting Game*, London, Abacus.

Staincliffe, C. (1997) *Go Not Gently*, London, Headline.

Stevens, A. (1996) *November Tree,* London, HarperCollins.

Turner, M. and Balloch, S. (2001) Partnership between service users and statutory social services in S. Balloch and M. Taylor (eds) *Partnership Working: Policy and Practice* Bristol, Policy Press, pp. 165–180.

Vine, B. (1996) *The Brimstone Wedding,* Harmondsworth, Penguin.

MARTILLAC - BRILLE CARDIFF. AC. UK

4

IMAGININGS OF AGE IN 1920s POPULAR NOVELS

Hannah Zeilig

There is little doubt that in the popular imagination, the 1920s is conceived of as a decade dominated by youthful ebullience.[1] In the collective historical memory, it is recalled as the 'roaring twenties': a time when gay young things danced the Charleston into the early morning hours. Young women 'flappers' wore short dresses and jazz music filled the dance halls. This is captured in the popular poem by Dorothy Parker:

The Flapper

The Playful flapper here we see,
The fairest of the fair.
She's not what Grandma used to be, ---
You might say, *au contraire*.
Her girlish ways may make a stir,
Her manners cause a scene,
But there is no more harm in her
Than in a submarine.

She nightly knocks for many a goal
The usual dancing men.
Her speed is great, but her control
Is something else again.
All spotlights focus on her pranks.
All tongues her prowess herald,
For which she well might render thanks
To God and Scott Fitzgerald.

Her golden rule is plain enough –
Just get them young and treat them rough.

As Jacques Chastenet has commented: '(The flapper) symbolized an age anxious to enjoy itself, anxious to forget the past, anxious to ignore the future' (1983). This desire to ignore the future and prolong youth was

reflected in one of the theme tunes of the era *Stay young and beautiful –
if you want to be loved*. Indeed, the 1920s was a decade when there were
more experiments with monkey glands to prolong youth than ever before.

CHALLENGING THE YOUTH CULT OF THE 1920s

Despite the associations made between the 1920s and youth, the
demographics of the period were characterised by an ageing of the
population. Census data for England and Wales shows that in 1921, 18.8
per cent of the population was over 50, while just ten years later that
percentage had risen to 22.3 per cent. Each age group from 50 to over 80
registered an increase between the census of 1921 and the census of 1931.
The decline in mortality, particularly infant mortality, coupled with the
declining birth rate, meant that more people were surviving into older
ages.[2] In addition, hundreds of thousands of young men lost their lives in
the 1914–18 war and the younger population was being depleted further
by the emigration of young men to the New World in the years following
the Great War. Hence, the 1920s was one of the first decades in history
during which worries began to emerge regarding the implications of an
ageing population. Indeed, it is arguable that the belief that an ageing
population might adversely affect the economy started in the 1920s,
fuelling the ageism of the later twentieth and early twenty-first centuries.

The need for higher pensions was a central concern of social policy
in the 1920s and 1930s. Apart from this, however, there was little public
interest during the 1920s in the position of older people in society.[3] The
paucity of social histories from either the period itself or
contemporaneously, examining anything other than the economic
situation of older people, is one of the reasons for looking to fiction for
further insights. Novels provide alternative angles for thinking about the
situation of older people in the 1920s and 1930s. Whilst we cannot claim
fiction to be fact, if we examine it carefully, it does make visible that
which other documents from the times have hidden. As has been noted by
Cockburn, a social historian, fiction can aptly capture a sense of the
times:

> Historians and sociologists must examine innumerable sources
> when they are in search of the mood, the attitude, the state of

mind of a nation or class at this or that period of time …. They also have to study what people said and wrote, as distinct from what they did. (Cockburn 1972)

With this in mind, I decided to turn to popular fiction to find out what it might reveal about ageing and older people in the 1920s.

1920s POPULAR FICTION: THE NOVELS STUDIED

In 1923 alone, 1,220 works of fiction were published. There are no accurate statistics of sales of fiction from the period and no statistics of total readership – so any attempt to gain a representative selection of 'popular' novels was futile. Instead, I found that social histories of the period which charted what people were reading together with contemporary reviews and bibliographies, were the most reliable means of discovering who was reading what. I then conducted a thematic analysis of six novels that presented fascinating characterisations of older people. A brief synopsis of these novels is as follows:

All Passion Spent by Vita Sackville-West was published in 1931, as the 1920s were fading into memory. Nevertheless, it portrays the period with poignancy. It is a unique novel above all for Sackville-West's sensitive portrayal of the protagonist, Lady Slane, who at the start of the novel is 88 years old. Her worldview is the lens through which the reader is invited to read the novel. Old age sounds a dominant note throughout the book, in which all but one of the characters are over the age of 60. Indeed, the atmosphere is that of a meditation on later life as it is experienced by Lady Slane.

The Old Ladies by Hugh Walpole was published in 1924 and is far from the best known of this prolific author's work. Told in the manner of a fable or a children's tale, the language is simple and there is a strong moral tone. The narrative centres upon three 'old ladies' (they are all in their early seventies) who live in rented accommodation. The narrative climax has two strands: the rescue (in a passage of remarkably purple prose) of one of the old ladies from potential destitution by her son; and the interactions between the other two older ladies. One of these is a particularly unpleasant character (Agatha Payne) who quite literally frightens her companion, May, to death.

To Let, the final volume of the first trilogy of *The Forsyte Saga* by John Galsworthy was published in 1922 and is the novel which most overtly captures the spirit of the 1920s. For instance the older generation are often revealed reflecting upon how different the 'new' generation seems. The narrative thrust of the novel is upon the fortunes of two older men – Jolyon and his cousin Soames – and their children. *To Let* provides insights into how older men negotiate relationships with their families.

Precious Bane, published in 1924, was a prize-winning novel by Mary Webb. Although set during times ostensibly far removed from the moment in which the novel was written, commentators have noted that this was to facilitate Webb's critique of the 1920s. My interest in the novel centred upon the older mother. Although she is relegated to the sidelines of the narrative, she features insistently and influences the plot substantially. After suffering years of what would now be termed abuse by her son and carer, she is poisoned by him. *Precious Bane* is also interesting for its critical insights into the position of women.

Hatters Castle by A.J. Cronin also features an older mother, who (as in *Precious Bane*) appears to be little more than an adjunct to the main story-line. However, her position within the familial hierarchy is interesting. She joins forces with her son (Brodie) to form a malign union through which they victimise Brodie's wife and children. By the end of the story, Grandma Brodie, as she is known, is the only character other than Brodie to remain living in the grotesque folly which is his 'castle'. The other character who I found interesting is Brodie's wife, who ages rapidly during the course of the narrative – until she is finally harried to her early death. As with *All Passion Spent,* although this novel was published in 1931, it harks back to the preceding decade.

So what can be extrapolated from these novels about ageing in the 1920s?

NOVEL NOTIONS – EXTRAPOLATING FROM THE PORTRAYALS OF OLDER PEOPLE IN THE NOVELS

The complications of family life for older people – especially older women

One of the themes arising most persistently from an overview of the novels is the extent to which family life is portrayed as being the opposite of a haven for older people. The older women, in particular, are portrayed as being trapped by the confines of their domestic spheres. In *All Passion Spent*, Lady Slane takes positive action to free herself from these confines. She rejects the demands and expectations that her adult children have for her old age, creating a new independence for herself:

> 'I am not going to live with you, Herbert, nor with you Carrie; nor with you William; nor with you Charles ... I am going to live with myself.'

Lady Slane, in her typically unconventional manner, refuses to be ensconced in the bosom of her family, as she is certain that it would be a less than comfortable arrangement. Similarly, Mrs Amorest, of *The Old Ladies*, although wanting her son to 'rescue' her, is keenly aware of the difficulties in her life to which he has contributed. Both these women are survivors despite their families rather than because of them.

Mother Sarn (in *Precious Bane*) is controlled by her son, she is at the mercy of his whims and when he finds that she is a burden – he kills her. Likewise, both women in *Hatter's Castle* are bullied by the patriarchal figure of Brodie and their lives are dictated by his tempers. Grandma Brodie is crucially reliant upon her son, who allows her extra food occasionally or relentlessly torments her for his amusement.

For all these fictional older women, family life is fraught with complications. 'The family' rarely provides support and is dominated by men who repress their older mothers or wives.[4] In contrast, the older men in *To Let* continue to control the financial purse strings and thus maintain some power within the family, even into later life. However, even in this novel, the family becomes an arena of conflict as the men age. This is particularly true for Soames, as his family is shown to be incapable of alleviating his sense of isolation or loneliness. Overall, in every novel family life is far from a source of any clichéd comfort for its older characters. Delicate balances of power and dependency have to be struck, at both the financial and emotional levels. The character of Lady Slane suggests that, for older women at least, it might be healthier to shun family altogether.[5]

Awareness that families may not be able to provide adequate support for their older members was beginning to surface in the 1920s. In this period, the debate about how best to care for older people was emerging and this included extensive discussion about where older people might live. This is equally a topic in current social gerontology. Not only has there been a steady growth of interest in the abuse of older family members but also historical research has shown that the family was never really a haven for its older members. Popular fiction, then, substantiates knowledge about older people in their families during the 1920s and also adds to this, as readers are invited to apprehend the consequences of how these situations might be lived by older people.

Looking at age

Feminist writing has illuminated the importance given to physical appearance for women and the extent to which this may be acutely experienced in later life. As noted by others, historically there has been one issue that stands out about ageing: the positive evaluation of youth in contrast to the revulsion and fear of ageing. Like today, culture in the 1920s revered youth and beauty with great intensity.[6] This was equally a theme which was highlighted by the novels. Another popular novel from the era, *Sorrell and Son* (Deeping 1927),[7] substantiates this point in the figure of an older woman who states, in tones reminiscent of a vampire:

> Yes, old age was detestable. She herself was on the edge of it, and her urgent vitality craved the young blood of youth.

The extraordinary good looks of Lady Slane in *All Passion Spent*, cast into stark relief the usual absence of any description of older women as aesthetically pleasing. Lady Slane retains both femininity and sexual allure far into her old age. In contrast, the older women featured in the other novels are depicted as small, physically withdrawn and asexual. For example, Grandma Brodie's increasingly masculine physical looks are attributed to her being a 'crone'. And when Agatha in *The Old Ladies* manifests signs of sensuality, it is conveyed to the reader as repulsive and a further sign of her depravity. The physical representation of older women in these popular novels reveals uncomfortable attitudes to the ageing process. The physical ageing of the older woman is either idealised, as in the case of Lady Slane, or more often vilified thus treating the characters as unsavoury or harmless.

In contrast, the older men in the novels are represented as having a physical continuity. In *To Let* for example, both men are married to women much younger than themselves; their sexual identities have clearly not been eroded in later life. Soames apparently,

> had not grown fat and flabby; his nose was pale and thin ... his eyesight unimpaired ... Little change had time wrought.

The physical processes of ageing are clearly less transparent for these men than they are for women. Little is different today, when women of increasingly young ages are urged to buy facial creams which might magically reduce wrinkles – whereas men, still manage to escape such intense pressures.

The relativity of 'age'

Above all, the notion that age can never be caught in simple formulas – including definition by chronological years, is highlighted in the novels. For whilst the decrepitude of the body may be a concomitant of later life, the character's emotional lives defy age categorisation. This is a powerful theme to emerge from the novels which raises wider questions, such as how we might 'know' old age and how 'old age' might be experienced. These are questions that were being asked with increasing frequency in the late twentieth century, specifically by those interested in the social construction of age (for example Gullette 1997; Hepworth 1997).

My analysis has highlighted the extent to which 'age' is a shifting variable. For instance, when a person might be defined as 'older' varies – as seems appropriate to their families. Grandma Brodie in *Hatter's Castle* is unequivocally an older woman but the extent to which her family stresses this depends mainly upon the mood of her son. He plays on her age as it suits him. Hence 'age' in these novels is an unstable predictor of a character's behaviour. It is an inconstant rather than a determined variable. Perhaps the most potent representations of the relativity of age versus the facticity of age are captured in the novels *All Passion Spent* and *To Let* in which the ageless, private core of each older character is revealed against the backdrop of their ageing.

The inherent contingency of age has been explored from a variety of angles in contemporary gerontological circles, including focuses upon images of ageing, the 'mask' of ageing and interpersonal definitions of ageing. It is a theme which is pertinent to current thought in social gerontology. This suggests a certain cultural continuity between the beginning and the end of the twentieth century; a century which has above all been notable for the ageing of the population and the concurrent grappling with what old age means. The notion that old age is a subjective experience and not simply an objective condition is at once the most important and the least surprising theme to emerge from these novels.

CONCLUDING COMMENTS

Of course one cannot make generalisations about the position of older people in the 1920s on the basis of six popular novels. Clearly any cultural artefact, such as a work of fiction, conveys a sense of its times which is also dependent upon the imagination of its author. There are many difficulties in trying to use fiction as data. However, the strengths of looking to popular fiction include its ability to communicate a taste from the era in which it was written. Fiction also attempts to vocalise those experiences that are commonly only felt or are left unlabelled. Most of all fiction taps our emotional worlds and these novels portray the private emotional worlds inhabited by older people. This aspect is frequently lacking in conventional sociological accounts of 'ageing' or 'older people'.

The themes highlighted by these novels demonstrate the continuities between the beginning and the end of the twentieth century. Thus we learn that then (as now) an older mother may not savour the prospect of living with her children, that for older women in particular the signs of physical ageing can be used to disempower them and therefore need to be fought against, and that for most older people the number of years they have lived is an unreliable guide to who they are.

NOTES

1. To a certain extent this is understandable. Following the Great War the younger generation were increasingly apt to challenge the older generation, who were widely regarded as 'out of touch with the times'. Indeed it is not surprising that it was towards the end of this decade that women won the vote on the same terms as their male counterparts (in 1928). What had previously been viewed as untenable and potentially subversive – that women might have a political voice – became acceptable.
2. Fewer people were dying in early adult life due to improvements in public health and the control of fatal diseases.
3. In accordance with the persistent sidelining of older people in general, they are largely absent from subsequent analyses of the period. As stated by Arber and Ginn (1991, p. 27), there is a need to re-evaluate the past in terms of the roles of older people.
4. This is most in evidence in those novels written by women: *Precious Bane* and *All Passion Spent*.
5. The sense of families in conflict threads through many 1920s novels. Disastrously unhappy families form the substance of most of Ivy Compton Burnett's work and are used to hilarious effect in *Cold Comfort Farm* by Stella Gibbons and feature in *The Orissers* by Leo Myers.
6. Advertisements for beauty products often portrayed fearful older women. For example, one such advertisement features the question 'Does your husband look younger than you do?' In the foreground is a woman with furrowed brow, anxiously looking over her shoulder at her husband who is otherwise engaged with a young woman. Another advertisement for 'Seventeen' – a natural beauty product – likewise contrasts an older and younger woman, the latter has the man's attention.
7. Incidentally this was also a bestseller in the US in 1925.

REFERENCES

Arber, S. and Ginn, J. (1991) Ageism and cultural stereotypes of older women, in S. Arber and J. Ginn (eds) *Gender and Later Life: A Sociological Analysis of Resources and Constraints*, London, Sage, pp. 33–49.

Chastenet, J. (1983) Europe in the Twenties, in J. M. Roberts (ed.) *Purnell's History of the Twentieth Century*, Harmondsworth, Penguin.

Cockburn, C. (1972) *The Books Everyone Read, 1900–1939*, Harmondsworth, Penguin.

Cronin, A.J. (1932) *Hatter's Castle,* London, Victor Gollanz.

Deeping, Warwick (1927) *Sorrell and Son*, London, Cassell.

Galsworthy, J. (1921) *The Forsyte Saga*, Harmondsworth, Penguin.

Gullette, M. (1997) *Declining to Decline: Cultural Combat and the Politics of the Midlife,* Charlottesville, University of Virginia Press.

Hepworth, M. (1996) 'William and the Old Folks': notes on infantilisation, *Ageing and Society* 16(4): 423–443.

Sackville-West, Vita (1931) *All Passion Spent,* London, Hogarth Press.

Walpole, Hugh (1924) *The Old Ladies,* London, Hogarth Press.

Webb, Mary (1924) *Precious Bane,* London, Virago Press.

5

'THE CHANGES AND CHANCES OF THIS MORTAL LIFE'
Aspects of ageing in the fiction of Stanley Middleton

MIKE HEPWORTH

INTRODUCTION

The title of this paper is taken from one of Stanley Middleton's novels, *Changes and Chances,* published in 1990. The quotation comes from *The Book of Common Prayer* where the *Collects After The Offertory* include the phrase: 'All the changes and chances of this mortal, life.' It seems to me to offer a particularly appropriate indication of the role of change and chance in making us more aware of the ageing process, either as perceived in ourselves or as observed in others. The act of reflecting upon changes in intimate personal relationships can stimulate an awareness of growing older and also give a particular quality to the experience of ageing. Similarly, chance encounters with acquaintances or strangers may contribute to age awareness and possibly influence self-reflection and personal life review.

At any period during the adult life course, the effort to make sense of the process of growing older does not take place in a social vacuum but is the result of encounters and conversations with other people. The excerpts I have chosen from Middleton's extensive fiction are intended to illustrate this social process. They show aspects of ageing as encountered by a number of his central characters (not all of whom are in the later part of life) during the course of their everyday lives. As sociological research into the ageing process shows, the experience of growing older is not simply a one-way process, ever more deeply into old age, but a sense of movement between the past, present, and future. In this reflective flow there is not one self within an ageing body (although this is certainly one way of experiencing ageing), but sometimes there is a poignant awareness of multiple selves: a self in the past, the present, and, no matter how limited it may be, the future (Hepworth 2000). The essential ambiguity of ageing is, therefore, that no individual can ever be categorised as merely old but as, for example, 'young-old' – in a stage of transition, of change and chance. Fiction, as a product of the creative imagination, provides valuable evidence of the validity of this insight, and the fiction of Stanley Middleton is an especially stimulating resource.

STANLEY MIDDLETON

Stanley Middleton was born in 1919 in Nottingham. He studied at Nottingham University, served in the armed forces during the Second World War, and has been a schoolmaster teaching English Language and Literature and then a headmaster. His first novel *A Short Answer* was published in 1958; his most recent, *Love in the Provinces* in 2002. He has to date published thirty-six novels and has earned the acclaim of critics including Allan Massie, A.S. Byatt, Bernard Levin, Isabel Quigly, and Ronald Blythe.

Middleton's novels take place in the English Midlands – Nottingham and district – described on the flyleaf of *Catalysts* (1994) as existing 'both in geography and in the imagination'. They are about the everyday lives of middle class people who are usually financially comfortable and have achieved respectable social status in the professions, such as teaching, accountancy, music, painting and writing. For this reason Middleton is often described as a 'provincial writer' who concentrates such close attention on the minutiae of everyday life that nothing much ever happens. But there is also critical agreement that the absence of a strong story is deceptive and that at another deeper level – the subtle realisation of reflective and reflexive interaction – his novels are extremely eventful. For example, in his review of *An After-Dinner's Sleep* (1986), Allan Massie wrote that the novel did not have 'a strong narrative, and of plot, in the strict sense of the term, there is none. Things happen, one after the other in lifelike manner: Murray's life (the central character who is aged 65) is composed of unconnected fragments.' Yet, he added, that these fragments come together in coherent form when perceived imaginatively through Murray's eyes. Through this literary construction, Middleton 'is wonderfully adept at giving one a feeling of the totality of experience. His characters live in a state of self-discovery and we readers have the pleasures of exploration' (Massie 1986).

In line with this interpretation, it can be added that Middleton's accounts of ageing and old age open up the reflexive nature of the ageing process by making it possible for the reader to trace the movements between social encounters, events and conversations and the subjective, privately concealed inner states of consciousness. The narrative of the story is from the perspective of the central character (always a man), who is often puzzled by what is happening or the significance of a particular conversation and is trying to make sense of what is happening. At the beginning, for example of *An After-Dinner's Sleep,* Alistair Murray, now retired and a widower, does not understand the reason for a sudden visit from Eleanor Franks. She is a former lover whom he has not seen for several years and this unexpected visit leads to a renewal of the affair, prompting in Murray a process of self-reflection and life review. This novel is centred entirely around the self-reflections and experiences of an older character who, in terms of the conventional western model of the life course, is in a transitional stage between youth and age.

Although ageing is a significant theme in Middleton's fiction, particularly his more recent work, this does not mean that his central characters are always older men or that old age and its consequences are the main focus of interest. In this discussion, ageing into old age from the perspective of the central character is a core theme only in *An After-Dinner's Sleep*. But, in addition to references to this novel, I have selected a number of excerpts from other novels by Middleton, which illustrate aspects of age-consciousness. The titles of these novels, in the order of their first appearance in this text, are: *An After-Dinner's Sleep* (1986); *Holiday* (1974); *Live and Learn* (1996); *Beginning to End* (1991); *Toward the Sea* (1995); *Changes and Chances* (1990); *Brief Hours* (1997). This paper is written in the hope that readers will be stimulated to read Middleton more closely.

In the excerpts, two kinds of encounter are of interest: firstly, chance encounters between total strangers who never meet again. These have been chosen as evidence of the way ageing can emerge as a topic of conversation. As such, these comparatively brief exchanges have a close resemblance to what Goffman describes as encounters: periods of face-to-face interaction when 'people effectively agree to sustain for a time a single focus of cognitive and visual attention, as in a conversation'

(Goffman 1972, p. 7). In Goffman's sociological analysis, encounters are sequences of social interaction where individuals search for information in order to make sense of what is going on. Evidence about the age of an individual, for example in the willingness to reveal one's age, is one significant source of information about the type of persons involved in an encounter and a significant stimulus of age-awareness. Personal age-disclosure or other sources of information about an individual's age are significant features of the interaction in several of Middleton's novels.

The second type of encounter is between people who are not strangers to one another, although it may be some time since their last meeting. This is a device Middleton favours, as for example in *An After-Dinner's Sleep*. Such meetings, of course, arise either out of a former relationship or as part of everyday family or occupational life. Because Middleton's central characters are always men, and the story is told from their perspective, occupational/professional life and the associations it produces are an essential part of the self-reflective narrative. However, it would be a gross oversimplification to argue that in Middleton's fiction ageing is seen only from a male perspective.

In the two kinds of encounter discussed in this paper there is sometimes a significant difference in age between the two people who meet: between a younger and an older man (*Holiday)*, between an older man and a younger woman (*Toward the Sea*), and between a younger man and an older woman (*Brief Hours*). Sometimes the interaction is between contemporaries (*An After-Dinner's Sleep*; *Brief Hours*), but in all cases these brief encounters, extended conversations, and longer-term relationships have been introduced into the narrative to explore the self-awareness of the central character and his attempts to solve a puzzle, resolve a crisis, and to come to terms with life. In Middleton's fiction, age disclosure and the experiences of time passing and of the ageing body are integral aspects of social events, interactions and reflections on experience that cumulatively influence the self-awareness of the central character. I shall now turn to a more detailed description of these two forms of encounter and discuss their relevance to an understanding of the meaning of ageing.

'CHANGES AND CHANCES'

In *Holiday,* Edwin Fisher runs away from a stormy marriage to the seaside town he used to visit in boyhood days with his parents. Fisher is from a middle class background and a lecturer in education. Wandering through the town, and cheered by the sights and sounds, he calls into a café and finds a seat opposite an older man, in whose appearance he shows only a passing interest. The older man does not sit in silence for long and, when he makes a remark about the weather, Fisher notices it is in a cultured voice. In the encounter which develops, there is a movement from routine conversation into self-disclosure on the part of the older man, who is thereby transformed from a stereotypical background figure – part of the scenery of the café – into an identifiable individual who lays claim to a distinctive, indeed socially influential, personal history.

As he is leaving the restaurant, the stranger concludes with a parting disclosure of his age:

> 'I'm eighty next,' he said, arriving, pulling car keys from his pocket. 'Feel it too, sometimes.' (p. 83)

In their research into the age-related language which emerges during the course of videotaped conversations between younger and old women, Coupland *et al.* (1991, p. 59) have drawn attention to the importance of 'age-categorization processes'. In these conversations, older women frequently disclosed their age to younger women to whom they were total strangers. The readiness of the older women to disclose their chronological age is described as a form of self-labelling or 'elderly identity marking' (p. 58) and is, the researchers argue, one of the ways old age or 'elderliness' is reproduced through talk. Telling one's chronological age to a stranger is one of the ways through which older speakers 'conversationally acquire elderliness' (p. 59). Intergenerational talk stereotypically includes the expectation of both younger and older participants that older people will reveal their age as a matter of course. In the view of the researchers, this expectation is one of the key mechanisms through which negative stereotypes of older people are created and sustained: 'they ... offer a dimension of interaction through which some doubtless well-intentioned younger interlocutors can draw out age-stereotyped behaviours from the old' (Coupland *et al.* 1991, p. ix).

In the example from *Holiday,* Middleton also utilises this process, although in his case disclosure of a specific chronological age comes at the end of the conversation when the older man has told some of the story of his life. Middleton begins with the stereotypical form of an old man who is simply part of the café background and then extends the interaction, seen through the eyes of the younger man, to more complex conversational interchanges leading to deeper levels of self-awareness in the principal character. Disclosure of chronological age comes in this sequence in the form of a coda: 'I'm eighty next...' (p. 83).

This encounter lingers on in Fisher's mind, prompting a closer reflection on the ageing process and old age. Although the older man has recounted certain details of his life and family circumstances, revealing that he has been a successful dealer in land and property and is well-connected, he never gives Fisher his name and, after he has taken his leave, the residual impression is sufficiently forceful to make Fisher consider asking a colleague, a historian, to find him the name of this person who has been prominent in local life. In addition, the stranger has told Fisher that although he is apparently healthy and well off, his wife has died and he believes that his sons are waiting for him to die to leave them his money. This information leads Fisher to realise that ageing into old age, the process of becoming an older person, can leave even those who are financially secure and who have led successful and influential lives 'unprotected' (p. 84), and he muses over the implications of the observation 'I never trained myself for old age.'

This brief encounter serves to highlight one of the central ambiguities of the experience of ageing, namely that it is both widely shared and yet a kind of unknown territory where seemingly everyone is searching for a map. The older stranger also serves to remind readers of the dangers of stereotyping and crude age-categorisation.

Strolling on the promenade, Fisher has a second age-related chance encounter, this time with old age pensioners on a bus. At first glance he sees them stereotypically as elderly passengers being shepherded off the bus by equally stereotypical 'middle-aged women in flowered dresses and cardigans' who shout loudly at their charges (p. 97). Shortly afterwards, in conversation with the bus driver, Fisher is given a brief glimpse of the inadequacies of collective stereotyping and the importance of discriminating between social groups and individuals:

> 'They've got some rum 'uns there,' the bus-driver said to Fisher. 'Some of 'em have no more sense than babies. One old fellow was going to have a pee in the middle of the bus. Had it out in front of these women. But most of them are as lively as you and me.
>
> 'The old fellow was weak in the head. Been inside a 'sylum, they said. Queer, in't it, how old age takes you? G'i me a nice, quick heart-attack any time. Over and done, then. Shock for them as is left, but I wouldn't like to be like some of these.' (p. 97)

In a single observation, the driver's words summarise the dilemma of collective stereotyping. On the one hand, some old people do suffer from biological and mental decline but on the other 'most of them are as lively as you and me'. Nevertheless, the driver's recognition of the possibility of a positive old age does not make it any the more welcome: 'G'i me a nice, quick heart-attack any time.' In this passage Middleton does not merely offer a trite reflection on the inevitability of biological ageing and the desirability of dying on time, his framing of the problem of the ageing body is integral to the novel's wider purpose of giving depth to Fisher's self-reflection and life review. In the case of *Holiday*, encounters with aspects of old age are constitutive features of the process through which he struggles, as a younger man, to come to terms with the death of his child and the breakdown in his relationship with his wife. These encounters are a cumulative influence on his perception of the course of his own life and his reflections on possible future courses of action which include the decision to go to see his wife.

Another example of an encounter between younger and older strangers occurs dramatically in the opening pages of *Live and Learn*. Here the central character is Jonathan Winter, who is in his late twenties and teaching at a university in the English Midlands. On his way home alone from a rugby club meeting he is confronted by four young muggers who pursue him into a cul-de-sac. In a kind of *deus-ex-machina* episode, Fisher is rescued by an older man, George Hookes, who hustles him into his house where he hides until the danger has passed. While inside, Hookes shows Fisher the shotgun he keeps in the house for self-protection. When he arrives safely home, Jonathan reflects on this episode and speculates on George Hookes' age and on the nature of his character as revealed in his behaviour and surroundings. In other words, Middleton uses this dramatically unexpected incident to prompt Jonathan into reflection about the ageing process.

Three significant issues concerning the meaning of the ageing process can be found in this example. Firstly, the association of ageing with risk: although both the younger and the older man are described as being exposed to the risk of serious assault in certain urban areas, the age of Hookes points up the specific risks to older people. Secondly, there is the question of determining Hookes' age. Hookes describes himself as 'elderly' but he may only be in his fifties. In other novels Middleton, adhering to a traditional model of the life course, has described the fifties as the beginning of old age, the point at which men in particular begin to consider retirement an appropriate and acceptable option (although Middleton is never simply what he seems and is keenly aware that chronological age is not the only factor when it comes to defining middle or old age). Thirdly, Hookes, whatever his 'real' age, is a rather unusual figure to encounter in an apparently provincial novel about middle class life. In his aggressive response and readiness for a violent mode of self-defence, he is closer to the raunchy ageing characters in films such as *Tough Guys*. The fact that he is out of doors in his shirtsleeves in the depths of winter, suggests physical resilience and challenge. As such he is quite different from Winter's father, described as a conventional middle aged, fifty-year-old chairman of Winter's rugby club. He is someone who justifies himself to Winter in terms of the traditional benchmarks of the 'entrance' to midlife 'decline' (Gullette 1997) which include a father dying of cancer.

In common with many other writers who are concerned with ageing and old age, Middleton provides vivid descriptions of the physical changes of the ageing body. But his interest in the interplay between images of the external appearance of ageing and descriptions of the subjective perceptions of the consequences, subtly shuttles the attention of the reader between past, present and future experiences of bodily change. Physical ageing undeniably produces a greater awareness of frailty and it is the relationship of the body to the self (or to the experience of multiple selves) which is the significant factor.

Beginning to End begins with a brief accidental encounter which draws our immediate attention to the vicissitudes of the body. Anthony Clark, a young teacher in a private school, is walking down the street when he catches sight of an older man in a state of collapse and struggling for breath. Clark helps him home and a relationship develops between him and Stapleton, the older man, aged seventy-five. A subsequent conversation between Clark and Stapleton's daughter suggests that Stapleton's problems with growing older are not simply physical in origin. His self-confidence is also at stake; he needs to talk with congenial others. A relationship develops uneasily between the two men, during the course of which Stapleton gives Clark his own complex view of the ambiguities of physical ageing. He describes his feeling that he is both well and unwell: he is clearly unreconciled with his ageing body. His perception of the relationship between the body and the self is coloured by a preoccupation with the contrast between the past and the present, and he finds it difficult to come to terms with the present. But almost at the end of the novel there are subtle signs that Stapleton may be changing and communicating more openly with his daughter.

Only two days after Stapleton has begun to communicate more freely with his daughter, he is dead from a heart attack and there have been no further developments in this tiny change in the relationship between father and daughter. And yet the tiny shift that has taken place in Stapleton's move towards more open self-disclosure is an indication of the emergence of a new possibility in later life: a small yet immensely significant move in the everyday moral scale of human interaction. As a member of an older generation of men who find it difficult to communicate with women, and especially daughters, Stapleton has gradually moved his ground as a result of his encounter with a sympathetic and helpful younger man. One message here is that, although age-categorisation may be relatively fixed in the public stereotyping of older people (Stapleton collapsed on the street is, at first sight, simply another old man who needs help), outward appearances conceal a more complex struggle with the self. Middleton, as a creative writer, is able to open up this dimension to his readers.

The complex interplay between social stereotyping and self-assessment can also be found in *Toward the Sea* (1995). Here there is another chance encounter, this time between two contemporaries who have not met for several years. The main character, Henry Shelton, a schoolmaster aged 59, is walking the street at night when a man calls out his name and introduces himself as Ted Naylor, a former schoolfellow. Henry has not recognised him and makes an excuse:

> 'My eyes aren't good in this light.'
> 'No. We're none of us as young as we once were.' Naylor's voice had a Midland twang. 'I come up this way to visit my mother. She lives on her own.'
> 'She must be a good age?'
> 'Ninety-three. And spry. You should hear her when we suggest she ought to have a flat or move into one of these warden-aided complexes. "I've lived here sixty-eight years" she says, "and I'll die here." They moved in when they were first married. It's where I was born. And I'm thinking of retiring next year when I'm sixty. I'm manager of Redgate's, the wood-yard in Basford.'

Henry Shelton sees himself 'trapped by late middle age' (p. 64). When he has yet another chance meeting in the park with Hempshill, an acquaintance who is a few years older and described as looking 'younger than his years', both are seen through Henry's eyes as 'on the verge of old age' (p. 107).

But not all people see Henry as old. His headmaster offers him full-time work which Henry refuses on the grounds that 'I'm nearly fifty-nine'. To this his headmaster replies: 'You don't look, or act like it' (p. 30). But what does 59 look or act like?

Previously he has been interrogated by a much younger woman, Helena, the daughter of the woman with whom he had a short affair when a schoolboy:

> 'Don't you have a regular woman friend?'
> 'I'm getting old, you know.' (p. 83)

Yet both Helena and the younger social worker Jennifer Speed, with whom he is having an affair, find him attractive, looking younger than his years.

In these comparative assessments, Shelton is seen through the eyes of differing characters as both younger and older: ripe for retirement in the eyes of some, young enough in the eyes of others to carry heavy occupational responsibilities and to pursue a vigorous and active sex life with younger women.

In social gerontology it is often argued that encounters between generations are problematic, and that conventional age-categorisations act as a barrier to mutual understanding. As noted earlier, the work of Coupland *et al.* (1991) shows how linguistic stereotyping shapes conversations between people of different generations and how age-stereotyping is actually brought to life during the course of routine conversations. Simon Biggs, in *Understanding Ageing*, is another gerontologist who has commented on 'the mutual suspicion of age cohorts (which) can so easily create a spiral of rejection and misunderstanding' (1993, p. 82).

Middleton's fiction provides ample evidence of such intergenerational stereotyping, but the great value of his accounts can be found in the skill with which he penetrates beneath the surface of conventional age-stereotyping in seeking the subjective meaning that lies beneath. As his stories unfold, he uses the facts of biological ageing in a range of encounters and extended interaction, to take the reader several steps forward towards a deeper understanding of the labyrinthine interplay of subjective consciousness and linguistic turns. And in his efforts to get beneath the surface impressions which are perpetuated in the formal processes of social interaction, there is more than a suggestion of masking and unmasking (Goffman 1968, 1971).

During an interview in the 1970s, Middleton described his outward appearance as that of 'a decent middle class old gentleman' who, on the inside, has experienced all the crises, difficulties and dangers of life, especially those in family life. This suggests that the ordinariness of Middleton's image is itself something of a mask and it is not surprising that *Changes and Chances* includes a paragraph where Stephen Youlgrave, a poet in his seventies who has just married Elsie, a middle aged woman, exuberantly labels himself in the third person as 'no stuffed shirt or a pedagogue':

> He's emotionally very deep and very volatile, I'd guess … But in limited fields. Literature explodes inside him, uproots him. And it needn't be 'a chorus ending from Euripides'; that hymn removed him from his wedding to some earlier time, and evoked emotion which expressed what he thinks or feels today's ceremony means. He was transfigured. That grey old man sitting there humming to himself was not only different from me and you, that's not too hard or unexpected, but from himself. Momentarily he was transformed because he brought together the powerful feelings of many periods of his life into one end at one moment. There were a dozen, fifty men and boys, all Stephens, fused into that one old heart. (p. 181)

For Middleton, the humdrum routine nature of social life conceals the turbulent struggle which gives the ageing process not only a particular subjective depth and moral significance, but also that existentially elusive quality that is so difficult for gerontologists to capture in conventional empirical research. Concealed by the outward appearance of each individual, and variously revealed to different audiences, is an extensive repertoire of age-identities or 'ages' of man and woman. Philip Davis, a perceptive critic, has argued in his review essay of *An After Dinner's Sleep* that, outwardly minimalising both himself and the scope of his fiction, Middleton is operating on a level of:

> 'deeper realism' which involves the recognition that 'life is mysteriously but "properly" a thing with something *deeper* behind it which while you are *in* it you cannot quite possess.' (Davis 1988, p. 38)

Alistair Murray's consciousness of ageing in *An After Dinner's Sleep,* is:

> 'the dilemma of a time of life very much "neither here nor there", baffled and confused in a minimalist present in between past and future, youth and age, here and there; present, indeed, but also nowhere.' (Davis 1988, p. 34)

Whilst Middleton works on an immediately accessible level of the traditional model of a biological process shaped by the socially structured 'ages' of childhood, youth, adulthood, middle age, and old age, he is also acutely sensitive to the fact that this apparently unyielding framework may often be a source of puzzlement to the individual and is open to question, negotiation and manipulation, even if this is on the smaller scale of changes and chances virtually imperceptible to outside observers.

In *Brief Hours,* the central character is Frank Stapleton, a successful accountant who has retired from full-time employment as head of his business. He is married to Thelma and their son's marriage to Francesca is going through a difficult time. In spite of the tensions, Frank and Thelma maintain friendly relations with their daughter-in-law's parents. Francesca's grandmother is aged eighty-seven; she lives in a private residential care home and is no longer able to communicate coherently. The older woman's dementia provides a talking point around which the fear of this 'condition' and its associations with ageing assume a greater emotive force.

In this novel, Frank is positioned between his son, daughter-in-law, grandchildren and the confused older woman in residential care. In adopting this authorial strategy, Middleton is clearly drawing on the traditional imagery of the 'ages of man/woman' and, in that respect, there is nothing particularly remarkable in this account. But a reading of the complete novel reveals this to be simply one amongst a number of reminders of age and change. These cluster around the central issue of puzzlement over the meaning of life which has haunted Frank since childhood. In another routine encounter, this time on the street with his neighbour, Dorothy Lloyd-Jones, whose car windscreen has been smashed by vandals, he asks if her husband will be upset by the damage to his car:

> 'I don't know. I don't think so. To tell you the honest truth it gives him something to occupy himself with. When he first retired, and that's more than ten years ago he was full of life and ideas and projects. But now he just seems to be waiting for something to happen to him. I sometimes say to him, "George, what are you hanging about for?" and he says, "The Grim Reaper."
> 'How old is he? If you don't mind me asking you.'
> 'Seventy-eight.' (p. 91)

'Waiting for something to happen' is a typical observation in Middleton's fiction. Financial and social success, material comfort, and membership of an extended family circle do not in themselves guarantee physical or psychological security in later life. Nor do they necessarily make sense of the ageing of the body and final death.

'THIS MORTAL LIFE'

In *Toward the Sea,* Henry Shelton is re-introduced to Marion Meeks, a former lover not seen for over forty years. She is very ill and he is shocked by her emaciated appearance which contrasts sharply in his mind with memories of her youthful sexual vigour. She tells him she would still have recognised him in the street after all these years, but privately he thinks he 'would not have recognised her, would have passed her in the street' (p. 13).

In his imagination Henry compares his memories with her present appearance. As a woman who 'flaunted her sex', she had broken the 'provincial conventions of love' and 'lifted him into an ecstasy beyond price' (p. 19). But 'now she was a smartly dressed skeleton with barely a word to offer him' (p. 19). And Henry never really finds out why Marion wants to see him again – is it because she is dying? The mystery lingers on. As gerontological research shows, interactions with older people often circulate around the ageing body and its routine associations with illness and death

The problem exemplified in the brief reunion of Henry and Marion, is how to relate to the ageing body; what kind of self to impute to the ageing and dying person. If we do not fully understand the self-perceptions of older people, then how do we adequately communicate? The ageing other will remain a mystery, a puzzle of the kind we can encounter in Middleton's fiction: a mystery continually provoking speculation and uncertainty concerning the interaction between the body and the self.

In certain respects Middleton's graphic descriptions of the vicissitudes and depletions of the ageing body are reminiscent of the *transi* of an earlier period in the western history of death: those disconcerting mortuary images of disfigured and decomposing bodies which served to remind viewers of the passing of time and the fleeting nature of this world's pleasures (Aries 1983). They are also reminders of inadequacies, missed opportunities and the possibility that the self is more than the mortal body – persisting dynamically in the endless quest for moral meaning in life, ageing and death. The imminence of Marion's death in *Toward the Sea* comes as a reminder that physical change and the process of gradual separation from the living, does not erase the memory of a former self or selves, or the persistence of the struggle for meaning through past, present and into the future. In this reading, the body and its self/selves are not necessarily one and the same; the experience of ageing is of a dualistic tension between the body and the self. This does not mean that body and self/selves can be separated essentially one from the other but that, as the record of imaginative literature shows, body and self may be experienced in later life *as if* they have an independent existence.

ACKNOWLEDGEMENT

An extended version of this paper was published in *Ageing and Society* (2001) 21(6): 721–737. The editor wishes to thank Cambridge University Press for permission to draw extensively on this version.

REFERENCES

Aries, P. (1983) *The Hour of Our Death,* Harmondsworth, Penguin.

Biggs, S. (1993) *Understanding Ageing: Images, Attitudes and Professional Practice,* Buckingham, Open University Press.

Coupland, N., Coupland, J. and Giles, H. (1991) *Language, Society and the Elderly: Discourse, Identity and Ageing,* Oxford, Blackwell.

Davis, P. (1988) 'A roaring whisper': review article of *An After Dinner's Sleep, Stand Magazine* 29(4): 31–43.

Goffman, E. (1968) *Stigma: Notes on the Management of Spoiled Identity,* Harmondsworth, Penguin.

Goffman, E. (1971) *The Presentation of Self in Everyday Life,* Harmondsworth, Penguin.

Goffman, E. (1972) *Encounters: Two Studies in the Sociology of Interaction,* Harmondsworth, Penguin.

Gullette, M. M. (1997) *Declining to Decline: Cultural Combat and the Politics of the Midlife,* Charlottesville, University of Virginia Press.

Hepworth, M. (2000) *Stories of Ageing,* Buckingham, Open University Press.

Massie, A. (1986) The oddness of ordinary lives, *The Scotsman*, 10 May.

Middleton, S. (1958) *A Short Answer,* London, Hutchinson.

Middleton, S. (1975) *Holiday,* London, Futura. [fp: London, Hutchinson, 1974].

Middleton, S. (tape-recorded interview, 1979) *My Work as a Novelist.* Library Education series: College of Librarians, Drake Educational Associates.

Middleton, S. (1987) *An After-Dinner's Sleep,* London, Methuen. [fp: London, Hutchinson, 1986].

Middleton, S. (1990) *Changes and Chances*, London, Hutchinson.

Middleton, S. (1991) *Beginning to End*, London, Hutchinson.

Middleton, S. (1994) *Catalysts,* London, Hutchinson.

Middleton, S. (1995) *Toward the Sea,* London, Hutchinson.

Middleton, S. (1996) *Live and Learn*, London, Hutchinson.

Middleton, S. (1997) *Brief Hours*, London, Hutchinson.

Middleton, S. (2002) *Love in the Provinces*, London, Hutchinson.

6

THE SARTRE–DE BEAUVOIR 'CONVERSATIONS' OF 1974
From life storytelling to age autobiography

MARGARET MORGANROTH GULLETTE

When Jean-Paul Sartre was 69, his worsening health and Simone de Beauvoir's fear that he might lose his ability to speak convinced her that the two of them should tape-record a 'dialogue' that would constitute 'a book about himself ... concerning [his] literature, philosophy, private life' (De Beauvoir 1984, p. 71). She learned how to use a tape-recorder and they began the sessions that year while on vacation in Florence and continued them in Paris in the fall of 1974. He died in 1980 and, in the following year, she edited these original, vigorously intelligent, intimate, spontaneous, poignant, and sometimes unintentionally funny interviews. The dialogues were published as 'Conversations with Jean-Paul Sartre' in the second part of a book called *Adieux: A Farewell to Sartre (La Cérémonie des Adieux)*. The book begins with her frank notes about the declines and intermittences of Sartre's final illnesses and the activities he managed to maintain in the last difficult decade of his life. This part was controversial: de Beauvoir was criticised for revealing her long-term partner's incontinence and private weaknesses.[1] Accusations of her treachery and defences of the sickness narrative have utterly overshadowed the 1974 conversations and most critics have ignored them.[2] Phyllis Rose is an exception: she finds the conversations 'vastly more interesting' than the first part, because she is interested in equality between Sartre and de Beauvoir as a couple (Rose 1985, p. 129).

   The 'Conversations' deserve to be read on their own. Only then can we ask why de Beauvoir put them at the end of *Adieux*. The two parts of the book complement each other, but they could scarcely be more different as narratives of a life course. In the decades since, biographies like John Bayley's *Iris* have taught the public that loving-kindness is not incompatible with posthumous reporting about a loved one's decline. Readers are less terrorised vicariously by representations of end-stage deteriorations, as we could be when AIDS, Alzheimer's and ALS

64

(Amyotrophic Lateral Sclerosis/Motor Neurone Disease) were taboo topics – too heavy for publishers to risk. Far from condemning de Beauvoir, we are much more likely to praise her long patience in caring for Sartre, her willingness not to wash her hands of him when he played her off against his other female nurses and the intellectual suitors for his final celebrity favour.

In any case, 'Conversations' has something else to offer to people in crisis, as well as to auto/biographers and age critics. One need not have any special interest in the two great French writers to find in their retrospect provocative ways of thinking about the life course and a compelling new model of life-writing.

Their conversations – no 'goodbye' about them – are as fresh as paint and constitute an astonishing auto/biography-*à-deux*. De Beauvoir was an ideal interlocutor. The questions she asked Sartre were based on their deep and continuous forty-year-long relationship. She had apparently as total a recall of his writings as he did, and she was curious and even pressing about the parts of his private life that she didn't know. She could and did correct him, jog his memory, sum up his positions, query harder, and remind him of connections between phases of his life. This was necessary, as he believed he had few memories, and those were 'commonplace [and] about three-quarters reconstituted' (p. 418). In short, she wonderfully used their reciprocal relationship to help him write an informal autobiography of his life, a sort of 'sequel' to *Les Mots*. That had been limited to his early childhood and he had never cared to continue it.[3] The gendered aspect of this relationship is that if *she* had been the one dying first, and the one who had abandoned writing autobiography early on, he would very likely not have made himself responsible for interviewing her.

Sartre, on his side, was in good form in those months of 1974. 'He could emerge, cheerful and intact, from abysses' de Beauvoir noted in wonder (p. 35). Initially he lent himself to the interviews out of ennui: 'since I've not a great deal to do at present, I have to take some notice of myself … otherwise I'd have nothing at all,' he said, witty in abjection (p. 176). But he soon became 'completely happy' (pp. 73–74). Their self-consciousness about speaking in front of future readers subsided. He responded readily. He must have been flattered at being so known, as any of us would be, in an arena (his own interpretation of his life) in which he of course had the last word on any subject. His voice was then dominant: the audiotape spun, and he had the right to refuse any correction or new direction she offered, or simply restate anything as he liked it. Often he seems to have been intrigued by her questions, and rightly so, because often they are strange new questions. Whether or not they were what Elaine Marks (1986, p. 189) calls 'the big, embarrassing questions', he answered most of them thoroughly. (De Beauvoir says she cut out the boring ones that provoked lackadaisical answers.) He didn't like superficial 'reminiscence'; they sidestepped that through persistent inquisitiveness. Most of the time he answered reflectively, but in plain sentences and unrhetorical language.

As published, this 330-page book is a special hybrid that gives new force to the double term 'auto/biography'.[4] Like all oral historians, de Beauvoir conferred life on her interviewee by capturing his views of his life course and times. But she had a posthumous role as well. Probably because they would come back to the same topic on different days, she 'rearranged [materials] according to their theme' (p. 131). She cut a good deal but says she did not change his words. If she got some kind of last word through reorganisation, we have no evidence of it. The virtue of the result is that his narratives about each of his selves have integrity. Considered as de Beauvoir's biography *of* Sartre, as arranged by her, it is a form of biography that many of us would like to construct with a beloved person, or, more sadly, would like to have constructed with our own dead while they were alive. The recognition of this fact could jump-start many a slowpoke into turning on a tape recorder and asking important questions.

At the same time, because Sartre was no anonymous witness, but an autonomous and world-famous political intellectual and writer, this is also an example of oral self-representation in collaboration with an other. Considered as an autobiography *by* Sartre, assisted by de Beauvoir operating as a smart and well-organised second self, this is the kind of record of a person's changes and continuities over time that many of us would like to have written or talked ourselves – both to have for our own use and to leave behind to others. It's a kind of heavenly-assisted life review.

As such, the document serves as a model approach to what in my book *Aged by Culture* (2004) I call 'age autobiography'.[5] This form assumes that your telling of your life course – the narrativising of your 'ageing' – always takes place in specific historical, economic and cultural circumstances: national, regional, gendered, racialised/ethnicised, classed and, above all, linguistic/mythical/narrative. You can understand your own implicit relations to age and ageing, and what forces mediate these relations, by examining your narratives. You needn't wait until seventy or a threat of illness to write age autobiography. It can potentially be written by any subject old enough to have seen a prior self fade and a new one emerge, and who cares to ask why. Age autobiography is a form we need to write in order to understand better the biased and backward age ideologies that do us harm, as creatures aged by the particular culture in which we chance to live. 'Conversations with Jean-Paul Sartre' is a rare example of joint work, a high-wire act. But if I can show it as an imitable process, this might open up life writing about age and ageing in exciting new directions.

ON KNOWING OUR NARRATIVES OF AGEING

The book is organised thematically, and within each theme more or less chronologically. Focusing on self after self – his body image, his sexual life, his sense of having an age, his reading, writing, and political career – Sartre and de Beauvoir swept through his life course. Sometimes this involved stopping at only two sequential ages (child and adult); sometimes they stopped at numerous ages. A reader learns to expect this structure, desire its suspense and crave its surprising variants. In such long-term chronologies, ageing is a constant which is never absent, even when age is not explicitly mentioned. Ageing, as I argue, is always a narrative (Gullette 2004, ch. 8). *Ageing* is also a vexed referent. In one of the commonsense, latent meanings of the term, it refers to the value of the passage of time. This is a value we determine not just in middle or old age, as some people unreflectively assume, but in any phase of the life course and about any experience that we can narrate. More exactly, the meaning of ageing depends on 'choices' made among the narratives on offer in your culture's particular repertoire of life-course imaginaries, including the body-related stories. Sartre's multiple mini-narratives thus constitute so many reports on his ageing. Critics who dismiss the conversations as repetitious have overlooked this important material.[6]

It is quite possible that a person's sense of the value of the movement of time might vary from year to year, or even from day to day, depending upon circumstances – historical, economic, physical, psychological, social. But Sartre had always believed in an underlying direction of value as de Beauvoir reminds him in her knowing, assertive way: 'There's one idea that has been very important to you – that of progress.' (p. 414). His reliance on 'progress' might have felt too dangerous to repeat, since Sartre was going blind and finding it very difficult to write. He had certainly despaired at times, and for all she knew he might have given up once and for all on progress as a narrative for himself. 'Ageing' is often reduced to one's illness, and then understood 'as a demonic force that terrorizes … and as hideous bodily confusion' (Woodward 2003). De Beauvoir had long understood ageing-into-old age that way, as Woodward has sensitively shown in another essay on her earlier work (Woodward 1988). Arguably, de Beauvoir was testing on Sartre a number of aspects of her long-held ageism, which was over-determined by her childhood anxieties and by the existentialist emphasis on the ability to maintain projects. In particular, de Beauvoir was testing various assertions about the old age of artists that she had published in her 1970 book, *La Vieillesse*. She had said there, in her no-two-ways-about-it style, 'But progress at this stage of life is of a disappointing kind' (1996, p. 409).[7] Perhaps in 1970 Sartre had agreed. Had his illnesses put many cherished beliefs into question? – that is the suspenseful question for those familiar with their philosophical ideas. But in 1974 he answers unhesitatingly.

> Sartre: Certainly. I thought my first books would be inferior to those that came after. I thought my main work would be completed by the time I was fifty and that then I should die. Obviously, this idea of progress came to me from the lessons in which progress was taught and from my grandfather who believed in it.

Sartre finds continuities in his selfhood, even with a comical younger self who thought he would die at 'fifty.' De Beauvoir presses him:

And from your choice of the future too. You think that tomorrow will be better than today. ...

Sartre: I thought that for me progress was concerned with form. It was a question of learning how to write better, how to acquire a style ... it wasn't a progress in knowledge. (p. 414)

De Beauvoir pushes him a little more. She goes abroad for an example of the most available antithesis to progress, the American view of ageing-into-midlife as a decline, exemplified by F. Scott Fitzgerald's *The Crack-Up*. She gives Sartre an opening to align himself with those who, whether declining in body or mind, find life a defeat. But Sartre proves stubborn.

De Beauvoir: It was a very optimistic outlook, compared with the attitude of all the many people who, like Fitzgerald for example, think that life is a process of disintegration – that the whole of life is a downfall, a defeat.

Sartre: I used to think that too. I thought it at various times in my life. Things that had begun and that ought to have been successfully carried out came to a halt. One therefore ended in failure.

De Beauvoir. The idea of failure is not the same as that of disintegration, of decomposition.

Sartre: That I never thought. I always thought life was progress up until death – *that it must be progress* [italics added].

De Beauvoir: What do you think about it now?

Sartre: The same thing. Progress does stop at some point before death because one is weary, because one is near senility, or because one has private worries. But by rights it should go on for a long time. Fifty's better than thirty-five....

As I see it, the moment itself is already progress. It is the present and it flows on toward the future, leaving behind it the poor, disdained, despised, denied past. For this reason I've always readily admitted misdeeds or mistakes, since they were committed by someone else.

De Beauvoir: You've always been steadfast in your life, both in your work and in your affections; but at the same time you don't possess any deep solidarity with your past. (pp. 414–15)

This exchange is by turns comic, scary, invigorating, and provocative. What is new is certainly not the simple notion of progress that declares 'Fifty's better than thirty-five', which positive ageing has made very familiar in the English-speaking world, and which has been generative to many novelists.[8] Sartre is far more eccentric than the gurus of personal progress dare to be. Life 'must be progress' he says sweepingly, although he had started by talking only about his own writing, not his whole life or the direction of some putatively universal life course.

Some readers may be startled by Sartre's apparent inability to put his sense of the necessary movement of time together with his own bodily degeneration. Is this what judgmental reviewers of other people's ageing narratives call 'denial'? He agrees that he thinks occasionally, 'I'm seventy: that is, I'm finished' (p. 418) … 'I thought about it yesterday, and last week too, or a couple of weeks ago' (p. 419). The whole exchange could also be read more eerily, as a life review written in a rather impersonal past tense, as if the speaking self had survived all the other selves. Sartre implies as much in explaining why he has so rarely had a sense of his 'age': 'So long as there was a future, one's age remained the same … But after sixty-five or sixty-six there's no longer any future … I'd said pretty well all I had to say' (p. 417). But this post human attitude is infrequent.

Everyone surely has the right to decide which of the ageing narratives available to them strikes them as the most fundamental. Decline or progress may be the only narrative imaginaries they have acquired from their culture, if it is western or capitalist, ageist and middle-ageist. Progress is the preferred elite choice between these two imaginaries – and not just for existentialists with projects. De Beauvoir had shown in *La Vieillesse* how necessary solid socioeconomic support is to a good old age. But even with financial security, progress can be a difficult narrative to maintain. Doing so, especially when ill health strikes, may take a lot of mental and psychological tricks.

Sartre's devices are startling even to a close student of progress narratives. He emphasises the corollary that Americans usually suppress, that personal progress requires 'leaving behind it the poor, disdained, despised, denied past' (p. 415). Then de Beauvoir caps his insouciant rejection of his inferior younger selves by observing, in the lofty language she had used also in *La Vieillesse*, 'you don't possess any deep solidarity with your past'.[9] (This may be true of many of us. The 'I' has a habit of *othering* past selves as strangers, while holding tight onto its right to say what they felt and said and did. Is that a description of all autobiography, or even a definition? Only a theory that includes being aged by culture could handle that paradox.)

People have the right to lie to themselves and even to their life partners. But I believe that Sartre's emphasis on progress was sincere, in that the devices were working well enough for him in 1974. Celebrities with a long-term stake in age hierarchy, not to mention some hope of literary immortality, have a great advantage over those of us whose sense of seniority is being continually weakened by a decline-obsessed society. (People with children who love them have access to a form of immortality.)

Other methods of Sartre's could work for others as preparation for moments of narrative crisis. Temperamentally anti-nostalgic, and aided by what we might no longer want to call a 'weak' memory, Sartre tends to etiolate his past selves. 'Yesterday is not sharp and clear', he says (p. 421). And de Beauvoir helps him hold on to progress from different directions by asserting: 'One can never realize one's age oneself – it is not present to us' (p. 417). She reminds him of several states of mind to which he has permanent access. A phenomenologist, focused on interior selfhood, has great advantages over people bombarded by social gazes that view them through harsh mirrors: specular beings inevitably decline. (A man who always thought he was ugly, as Sartre did, has less to lose.) A busy political person – whose 'consciousness is directed toward the outside world and not toward your state … [not] toward an image of yourself' – also is freer. And then she blithely adds a non-Freudian notion of continuity: 'You've explained that fifty times. The ego is not in the consciousness, and the consciousness is therefore always perpetually present, fresh, unchanged' (p. 420). In his narrative crisis, Sartre's latest version of existentialism can be seen, unexpectedly, as a life vest, fully plumped up against decline.

The two of them run through his life course so many times that it becomes a habit for the reader, to expect that each new aspect of Sartre's identity (lover, writer) must have its own longitudinal story – what I call an 'age identity'.[10] His have this distinctive quality: that they do not fall into a single repetitive pattern. If one identity started in childhood, another started in his thirties. Nor does his life course fall into stages – Eriksonian, Jungian, Sheehyan, or any other. If one self changed drastically in his teens, another changed only at fifty, or at sixty-five, and then not because of his age but because of what he coincided with: a friend reading a new kind of novel, getting put into a German prisoner-of-war camp, or no longer believing he had anything left to write.

There is only constantly a story to be sought – about him as a reader (why he gave up reading novels) or as a sexual being (why he always preferred to reject 'what is strictly called sexual pleasure' [p. 315]). There is always the chance that a sounding will reveal something odd and unexpected. He had a body which in his imagination was 'fit and capable of all sorts of exploits' (p. 313) – that of an action hero – but which was in adult reality comparatively small, timid and easily fatigued. When they talk about whether as a child he minded being small, he says he always had 'an adult imaginary body' (p. 321). But at the same time he doesn't think of himself as an adult male. Discovering contradictory simultaneity – 'breaking the bones inside his head' (p. 3) – was itself pleasurable.

Despite their pact to defend the importance of progress, Sartre's age identities are not all progress narratives. The book opens, at de Beauvoir's instigation, with a formidably long list of works he left unfinished, in which the word 'failure' comes into play, although in no conclusive fashion. In other cases – his body image, or his relations with women over time – a pattern, having been set in the past, remains quite inert. 'I think I was always very protective and therefore imperialist' with women who were not you, he says to de Beauvoir (p. 298). 'But the sexual act – it existed too, and I performed it. Indeed I performed it often; but with a certain indifference' (p. 302). Fixed patterns too may assure a self – a self that doesn't like change – that it is 'ageless'.

Sartre's many mini-narratives confirm the theory that we have multiple selves (even if we happen to notice that he had more selves, and more definite ones, than most of us do, and even if we suspect that some he was very likely constructing while they talked). Reading the series can also convince us of something new: that in complex life storytelling, many kinds of ageing narratives coexist, however inconsistent in theory. There can be some selves in fixed patterns, in tandem with linear selves moving along progress or decline trajectories. There can be selves still changing, or initiatives that project change. Progress is compatible with continuity.[11] Progress narrative, I would add, is a capacious genre. It can be rich enough to contain a certain amount of failure or decline, and tones other than the upbeat – jeremiad, satire, lyric and the blues, and tragedy. A *complet* need not even have a dominant note. Sartre's auto/biography, to my sense, does not finally offer an insistent 'underlying' genre, even though he found himself looking back on his whole long variegated past with 'a benevolent eye' (p. 400).

We are lucky to have such an auto/biography, expanding the range of possible narrativisations of ageing. The vivid sense it gives of multiple, contradictory processes seems to me also a strength for *Adieux* when both parts are considered together. The first part of the book is that diary of the other, written by the caretaker, the shocked viewer of the once-beloved and now wasting body, who admires his resilience and political energy but cannot help but record physical decline. Whether she wanted revenge or was torn by pity, we'll never know her motives for publishing the diary.[12] But then against it, and after it, at twice the length, de Beauvoir set the other, larger part of the book – written by a person in the midst of a physical crisis who as he speaks does not feel that dying is his future. She allowed him to have the last word, and this is what it turned out to be. He convinced her so well that he was living that even much later she hesitated too long to ever tell him he was 'dying'.

The benefit of this structure is a lesson about the words 'living' and 'dying'. Where the-other-who-is-terminally-ill is concerned, the rest of us seem to need repeated proofs of where the emphasis must lie. Sartre's attitude is not easily labelled. Neither 'transcendence' nor 'denial' fits well. 'Conversations' tell the way it feels to an active speaker to be alive now, through storytelling, with the whole curious sweep of his life to run through at will, and a real challenge latent throughout the encounter, to square his story with his life partner's knowledge. No wonder that Sartre, in the midst of a disintegration he certainly knew from within, was at times happy. Telling autobiography honestly and critically – producing some new form, something unnamed that can be called age autobiography – may be an action that by the same token produces the vital, the fascinating, the engagé.

ON DISCOVERING OUR SOURCES

Not only did Sartre know his own dominant narrative genre, but he knew where it came from originally. 'Progress' came to him in childhood from being French and his grandfather's grandson. As a schoolboy, he had been taught the thinking (romantic/ evolutionary/populist?) that over-determined how a life-course trajectory should be interpreted: as a meliorist project. Turning back to ask about his sources happens so often that it is like a tic. He knows why, in lycée, he had felt he had to 'follow the program' of wanting 'amorous relations with scores of women', just as his friends did. 'I learned that from the books devoted to the great writers' (p. 294). 'I no longer really see why people write novels' says the author of *La Nausée*, and proceeds to ask why. 'There must be an explanation of what it means to become apolitical', he reasons (p. 374), so the two travellers tromp through that former self and a whole later set of events, his engagements with history.

A more critical genre of self-writing is made possible by the fact that people can work on their own naive autobiographies to discover more about their acculturations – including how they have been aged by culture, starting with the prospective narratives told to them in childhood.

Most people, perhaps even most age critics, have little idea that ageing is a narrative based on particular cultural imaginaries, brought by us into plausible close relation to our particular life conditions. Unlike Sartre-cum-de Beauvoir, most of us probably cannot say off the bat what our narrative genre is, how it was originally constructed, whether it changed over our life course and why, whether it is consistent with our other self-narratives, or how it might resist when tested by challenging events or discourses. Might we have a better idea of a friend's predominant genre – or of our parents' – than our own? Did de Beauvoir know her own or only Sartre's? We other mortals may have to work, to make such discoveries. And we are not all able to attract long-term loyalty from a person with an intact memory of our bodily history, our friends, and our thoughts.

Fortunately, age autobiography does not depend on such privileged conditions. It's as well to point out that from an age-studies' point of view, their interrogations too ended short. Sartre did not always stop to consider the contingent relationship between his various selves and French culture and history. He says, delightfully, about having eaten 'vast quantities' of *charcuterie* throughout his life, that sausage-eating 'obviously comes from' his Alsatian background, 'but does this explain it? That's another matter' (p. 317). A search for continuity even of an apparently trivial sort could enhance a philosophical inquiry about 'change'. But as a detective of a metasocial sort, Sartre can be unhelpful, either because he took his conditioning for granted (in, for example, wanting scores of sexual relationships) or contrariwise, because he wasn't ordinary enough.

De Beauvoir, on her side, could have asked him many more questions about ageing and his narratives, and age in his narratives. In an earlier interview about his body image, he had said, 'I'm more or less settled into my fifties. In other words, the man who goes downstairs at home, who walks along the street, seeing people and greeting them, is a person of fifty. In fact, I rejuvenate myself by twenty years' (p. 324). De Beauvoir didn't bring this up later. She didn't ask him 'Why *fifty*?' but an age critic would have to. 'And you said that when you were younger you expected fifty would mark the start of political life for you, and also that you expected to stop writing and to die at fifty. Why was "fifty" so variable, and yet was and is so central to your life storytelling?' Why does Sartre say that in terms of experience he is still 'thirty'? Why is rejuvenation so automatic for someone with such a good fix on progress?

What were the symbolic effects, if any, of '1968'? It was in fact not only a student movement but also a movement of unionised workers. However, as in the United States, 1968 came into the French political imaginary as a 'youth-movement'. This had devastating effects on some French people, then in their middle years, perhaps above all intellectuals and political people, who might otherwise have expected to age into seniority rather than decline. Jean Améry, a concentration-camp survivor who was settled in Paris by 1968, said it was worse to grow old than to have been in Auschwitz. De Beauvoir could have asked Sartre whether his interest in Maoists, as opposed to Communists, had anything to do with the cachet of the young politicos versus the 'Old Left'. She could have asked, 'If you believe in progress as the movement toward the future, isn't it dangerous to connect 'youth' with 'the future' in any exclusive way? Won't that doom all of us universally as we age beyond a certain age?' The 'Conversations' do suggest how newcomers might write a more critical auto/biography, but only up to a point.

De Beauvoir can be called the godmother of age studies. In *La Vieillesse*, she had advanced the thesis that old age 'is not solely a biological, but also a cultural fact' (1996, p. 13). Yet she could not go far enough toward age studies, toward denaturalisng their own culture and their historical moment and Sartre's internalisations. The imaginary body of old age, which to her, some critics think,[13] was a feminised declining body, may also have got in her way. Nor could Sartre 'think against himself' as much as these conversations now provoke us to do. But to be fair, even decades later, after much work in feminist, humanistic and critical gerontology, we all have blind spots about age and narrative and therefore miss important subjective and cultural elements of ageing, the life course and the staging of life. Of the three allegedly body-based categories – age, gender and race – age remains the least scrutinised, the one most buried in body and least troubled by theories or movements antagonistic to positivism.

If de Beauvoir had been able to ask more age-wise questions of Sartre in 'Conversations', she would have become not only a generic age critic, but also an age autobiographer. In *Aged by Culture*, I personalise this age autobiographer as a female muse of the new form of life writing. She erupts into chapter 8 'From Life Storytelling to Age Autobiography' with a theory cap on her head and a tart tongue in her mouth. She barges on stage scolding feminists, gerontologists, cultural critics, and professors of Youth Bildungsroman, for ignoring age. Then she settles into her stride by correcting my account of how my sense of being a 'woman' changed from age seventeen through my forties and fifties. This isn't nastiness on her part, but heuristic assistance. 'One road to autobiography critique is to show what's missing in the writing of others, as I began to do on Margaret's story of being a Woman-over-time. I didn't do this to prove her "wrong", only to show how much more context she could have given' (Gullette 2004, p. 152). Age autobiography is a complex life-course narrative plus an age-wise critical commentary about being aged by culture.

Once we have begun to theorise the form, we can see how democratically open it is. If we have an age autobiographer like Simone de Beauvoir to help us, great. If we do not, the single primary prerequisite is always at hand internally. The person who possesses the most privileged information about me, potentially, is *me*. I can talk into a tape recorder or sit at a desk alone, rightly acting as if I have a listener who is insatiably curious about my past and willing to embrace whatever the investigations of my latest self turn up. The pursuit is open to anyone willing to investigate the intersections between her original shaping sources and her unique freedoms, over some part of her life course. Through such critical reflectiveness, we each begin to practice being our own age autobiographer.

What feminist autobiography is to being sexed and gendered, and auto-ethnography is to being othered by race or national origins, age autobiography will be to being aged by culture: the revealer of the conditions of discourse. Writing the new form will have its own difficulties. But trying to solve them puts us on the road that leads to understanding our multiple and sequential selves, not as static or isolated from others, not as determined by our chromosomes, nor as dominated by our final ends, but as embodied psyches in culture over time, telling our stories as best we can.

NOTES

1. She was charged with appropriating his voice and his life, with voyeurism, and with desires for revenge.
2. De Beauvoir herself confused readers by writing, 'The ceremony [of goodbye] lasted ten years; these are the ten years I tell about in this book' as if *only* the illness narrative were in 'this book'. Quoted in Idt (1991, p. 367).
3. Tidd calls it a sequel 'although he does not uniquely determine the focus of the conversations' (1999, p. 169).
4. Liz Stanley's much-used term usually means that autobiography can't be written except inter-subjectively, incorporating one's parents or others. Sometimes the term alludes to particular auto/biographies

that blur the two genres – like Henry Adams's, written in the third person. There is a need for such a term, even if it over-emphasises the difference between self-writing and writing about an other.

5. Gullette, M. M. (2004), pp. 18, 20, 27, 121–39, 142–43, 152. My recent reading of the second half of *Adieux* enables me to develop further a few key concepts from chapters 7 and 8 of that book and from an entry on age studies (2000a).

6. Elaine Marks made the wonderful point that the tendency to read the illness diary psychoanalytically led to overlooking 'le vécu' (experiences such as aging, declining, and death) but after praising Beauvoir for this transgression, she says nothing further about the conversations (1986, p. 189).

7. De Beauvoir must also have heard how he moved from her present tense ('You think that …') to what he had thought in the past, as if he had changed his mind.

8. I describe progress narrative in *Safe at Last in the Middle Years* (1988) and in *Declining to Decline* (1997).

9. In *La Vieillesse* de Beauvoir creates a binary between the mass of old people who cling to a more youthful past self nostalgically, versus the superman whose project is 'to advance' beyond 'the self he is no longer' (*The Coming of Age,* 1996, p. 362).

10. See Gullette, M. M. (2004), chapter 7, 'Age Identity Revisited'. Chapters 7 and 8 define the relationship between age identity and age autobiography.

11. There is some explanation of this in Gullette M. M. (2004), chapter 1.

12. Bainbrigge says in a footnote that 'the inclusion of the author's interviews with Sartre preserves his voice and presence in the text' and is a sign of empathy (2002, p. 839 n. 23).

13. Jardine, A. (1986), p. 93; Marks, E. (1986), p. 14.

REFERENCES

Bainbrigge, Susan (2002) *La Cérémonie des adieux* and *Le Livre brisé*: situating Sartre in the text, *The Modern Language Review* 97(4): 835–849.

De Beauvoir, Simone (1984) *Adieux, A Farewell to Sartre* (tr. by Patrick O'Brian), New York, Pantheon. [fp: *La Cérémonie des Adieux*, Editions Gallimard 1981].

De Beauvoir, Simone (1996) *The Coming of Age* (tr. by Patrick O'Brian) 2nd edn, New York, W.W. Norton, [fp: *La Vieillesse,* Editions Gallimard 1970].

Gullette, Margaret Morganroth (1997) *Declining to Decline: Cultural Combat and the Politics of the Midlife*, Charlottesville, University of Virginia Press.

Gullette, Margaret Morganroth (2000a) Age studies, and gender, in Lorraine Code (ed.) *Encyclopedia of Feminist Theories*, New York, Routledge.

Gullette, Margaret Morganroth (rpt. 2000b [1988]) *Safe at Last in the Middle Years. The Invention of the Midlife Progress Novel*, www.iuniverse.com

Gullette, Margaret Morganroth (2004) *Aged by Culture*, Chicago, University of Chicago Press.

Idt, Genevieve (1991) Simone de Beauvoir's *Adieux*, in Ronald Aronson and Adrian van den Hoven (eds) *Sartre Alive*, Detroit, Wayne State University Press, pp. 363–384.

Jardine, Alice (1986) Death sentences: writing couples and ideology, in Susan Suleiman (ed.) *The Female Body in Western Culture: Contemporary Perspectives*, Cambridge MA, Harvard University Press, pp. 83–96.

Marks, Elaine (1986) Transgressing the (in)cont(in)ent boundaries: the body in decline, *Yale French Studies* 72: 180–200.

Rose, Phyllis (1985) *Writing of Women*: *Essays in a Renaissance*, Middletown, Wesleyan University Press.

Stanley, Liz (1992) *The Auto/Biographical I*, Manchester, Manchester University Press.

Tidd, Ursula (1999) *Simone de Beauvoir: Gender and Testimony*, Cambridge, Cambridge University Press.

Woodward, Kathleen (1988) Simone de Beauvoir: aging and its discontents, in Shari Benstock (ed.) *The Private Self: Theory and Practice of Women's Autobiographical Writing*, Chapel Hill, University of North Carolina Press, pp. 90–113.

Woodward, Kathleen (2003) Telling time: aging and autobiography, *Generations*, forthcoming.

7

CONCLUSION

JULIA JOHNSON

The five papers here have taken us down many roads. So, in attempting to draw together some conclusions, it is perhaps worth returning to the question posed in the introduction to this collection: 'How might we better understand ageing through fiction and other forms of creative writing, and what tools for analysis does such literature furnish us with?' One way to address this question is to consider these papers in terms of two related issues: context and meaning.

CONTEXT

Although it is important to look at narratives, be they poems, fiction or personal biographies, in terms of their internal consistency, we have always to remember their historical, social and cultural context and, indeed, the significance of who is writing and what their intentions and motives might be, acknowledged or otherwise. As Andrew Blaikie pointed out as discussant at the original seminar, we cannot get off the hook, if you like the sociological hook, of thinking about contextualising what is produced. And, as Margaret Morganroth Gullette's paper makes clear, all narratives are culturally produced and 'ageing is a narrative based on particular cultural imaginaries'. So, what we might learn about ageing is tempered by context and the papers here amply demonstrate this.

For example, Joanna Bornat contextualises the public appearance of *Kate* in the community writing movement of the 1960s and 1970s. It was a time when the voices of ordinary people started to be championed. It was also a time when institutions for vulnerable groups in Britain, including older people, were subjected to a great deal of public scrutiny and criticism and, as a consequence, there was a growing concern to improve institutional practices and combat the depersonalisation so characteristic in institutional settings.[1] This concern has not gone away and, whatever one might think of the literary merits of the poem, it remains relevant and powerful for care workers today. The novels reviewed by Jill Manthorpe were all written in the 1990s reflecting contemporary concerns about residential care in a context in which nearly all care home provision in Britain has moved into the hands of the 'independent' sector[2] which arguably is less open to social researchers. It is also, as Manthorpe points out, a highly gendered context – one which is predominantly occupied, visited and serviced by women and one which women authors are writing about.

Hannah Zeilig reviews novels written in the aftermath of the First World War: a context in which people wanted to 'forget the past, enjoy the present and ignore the future', when there was an acute shortage of young men and when the population was ageing. In such a context, the imperative for women to 'stay young and beautiful', together with the relegation to the sidelines of older women, is hardly surprising. But it was also a time when women were achieving political rights and independence. In addition to contrasting the way in which older men and older women are physically portrayed in the novels, Zeilig contrasts the physical portrayal (by Vita Sackville West) of Lady Slane with the physical portrayal (by other authors – some of whom are men) of the older women in the other novels. These contrasts suggest that power and independence had to be dissociated from the physical signs of ageing.

Apart from the social, cultural and historical context, there are also the intentions and motives of the authors to be considered. What is so fascinating about the poem *Kate* is that we do not know who the author is and therefore whether it is a piece of fiction, biography or autobiography. Arguably, fictional accounts offer the greatest scope for saying what needs to be said and revealing 'the truth' because they are not constrained by the need to produce documentary evidence. Paradoxically it is the anonymity of *Kate* that gives the poem such power: it is the ultimate representation of the real person trying to get out from behind the mask of ageing. If we were to be told that the author was in fact a nurse, that it was simply a piece of imaginative writing, it would lose its authenticity, and possibly its power. So, the anonymity of this poem may be an artefact but perhaps one that it is best left undisturbed.

Margaret Morganroth Gullette's paper specifically addresses the issue of motive and points to those who may argue that de Beauvoir was seeking revenge in revealing the intimate details of Sartre's physical decline. Likewise, eyebrows may be raised at the intimate revelations in other auto/biographical writings, such as those of John Bayley[3] and Margaret Forster.[4] Most of us are grateful, however, for what we have learnt from these writings and their authenticity lends them much power. Nevertheless, in auto/biographical writings questions remain about what has been included and omitted and in particular why.[5] As Thompson et al comment in relation to mid nineteenth century autobiographies: '… what they omit or include is in itself evidence of the attitudes of the writers and of the readers they had in mind' (1990, p. 45).

So, gerontologists who turn to fiction or other forms of creative writing to learn about ageing need to give serious consideration to the matter of how what they are reading came to be written. But they also need to give attention to another aspect of context – form – and consider why a particular form has been adopted and what it has to offer.

The writings reviewed in this collection include a variety of literary forms – poetry, novels, biography and autobiography – and a variety of literary genres and styles. They were also written at different times ranging from the beginning to the end of the twentieth century. The theme of ageing is mediated through these different forms, styles and periods and as gerontologists we might ask what opportunities and constraints they offer in our endeavour to understand ageing.

In the poems and novels, the figures we are looking at have a fictional landscape, which in itself is a structure that can be constraining. Some of the fiction reviewed here, because it is popular, is accessible, and because it is accessible it is not breaking the rules in a way that avant-garde poetry or other forms of creative writing have done. As a result we can get left with clichés and with stereotypes – the people who wear purple and so on. Andrew Blaikie suggested that there may be a great deal of literature to do with ageing that we will never see because it does not strike a chord with many people and so it is not available on the bush telegraph or through the kind of round-the-world chain letter such as with the poem *Kate*. So if something does not strike a chord, a popular chord, it may never be revealed for us. Nevertheless, if something is striking a chord, then there is something there in the imaginative empathy, or call it what you will, that we really ought to explore.

But different forms of creative writing can produce a huge number of convincing possibilities – ways of thinking about possible futures for ageing and ways of trying to make sense of something that is difficult to write about. This relates to genres of literature, such as science fiction, crime fiction or perhaps magical realism, which may not be so constraining. Andrew Blaikie recalled that Doris Lessing once said in a lecture that she writes science fiction because it seems to be the only way in which she is able to imagine and think about other possibilities: it has offered her new ways in which she can express herself. Kurt Vonnegut's *Tomorrow, Tomorrow and Tomorrow*[6] is a classic example of how popular science fiction has been used to visualise ageing in the future.

MEANING

As mentioned in the introduction to this collection, creative writings are a potential source of understanding what ageing and old age mean. In seeking meaning, we need to take into account the interaction between ourselves as readers and the text we are reading. Joanna Bornat describes the contrasting reactions of readers to the poem *Kate*. This alerts us to the fact that not only do different readers draw out different meanings from what they read but also the same reader finds new meanings at different points in time.

Shortly before she died, Carol Shields wrote about rereading Muriel Spark's novel *The Girls of Slender Means*, which she first read in 1963:

> I was in my 20s when I read *The Girls of Slender Means* the first time, and so 'related' to the young women who occupy its pages. This was during a period in my reading life when I was given to understand that 'relating' to the fictional characters or situation was of prime importance, and so I read, I'm sorry to say, narrowly, frugally, unadventurously, as though I had no interest in the greater world and no desire to experience other cycles of thinking and being. ... Naïve as it may sound, one read fiction in order to confirm the reality of one's experience. (Shields 2003)

On rereading the novel forty years later, Shields found that what she had remembered as a 'light' and 'girlishly jolly' book was 'a deadly serious work of art'. She describes the girls' slenderness as being not so much in their means as in their 'half-perceived notions about what their lives will become and their overestimation of their power in the world' and their situation as 'tinged, almost from the first page, by a slowly mounting sense of damage and death'. She concludes that on her first reading of the novel, she was so occupied with 'relating' that she missed these 'careful clues and warnings'.

It is worth thinking about the contributors to this collection and what literature each has chosen as their focus. It is also worth thinking about our own choices and potential interpretations – what are we seeking in terms of age from the literature we read, and why? How do we position ourselves in relation to the text?

Blaikie suggested that an elusive and puzzling quality in so much of the writing about ageing is an attempt at self-discovery that may not get very far, but the actual journey – the travelling – appears to be what is important. Travelling is a metaphor often used in connection with ageing – the idea of life as a journey, or as an odyssey. In a sense, he suggested, we are trying to spatialise something which is temporal, which is time-related. The issue of non-linearity, however, comes into play also. Ageing is a process of reflexive interaction of becoming, of reflexivity, of seeing things beneath the observable and so on. It is not necessarily linear, so the pattern that emerges from all this may be a very confusing pattern, one that is replete with contradiction, but nonetheless it is some kind of pattern. All writing, like any form of communication, relies upon symbols and we ought not to forget that when we are looking at creative writing about ageing we are reading symbolic attempts at explaining ageing and the life course. So we might look at a particular novel and ask what symbols might we derive from it which seem to relate to ageing, whether they are to do with paths, with journeys, with comparing the life of humans with the growth of plants or whatever.

Middleton's novels arise out of his own middle-class Nottingham background and, as Mike Hepworth has suggested, in them the characters embark upon a journey of self-discovery. We might speculate therefore that Middleton has used his fictional characters to write his own ageing. The conversations between de Beauvoir and Sartre, however, are an explicit form of life review and are unusual perhaps in the specific attention they give to age. Bytheway in his analysis of the letters and diaries of Mary Berenson demonstrates how much there is to be learned about how people theorise age through ordinary talk and writing (1993a, 1993b). Likewise here Margaret Gullette suggests that Sartre's mini-narratives are ageing narratives. She suggests too that they provide an initial template for every one of us to consciously write or record our own age autobiography. But whether the dominant narrative genre of our age autobiographies will be 'progress' remains to be seen.

NOTES

1. A stream of research literature was produced at this time which became known as the 'anti-institutional literature'. It included: Barton, R. (1959) *Institutional Neurosis*, Bristol, John Wright; Goffman, E. (1961) *Asylums*, London, Penguin; Townsend, P. (1962) *The Last Refuge*, London, Routledge and Kegan Paul; Robb, B. (1967) *Sans Everything*, London, Nelson; Morris, P. (1969) *Put Away*, London, Routledge and Kegan Paul; Meacher, M (1972) *Taken for a Ride: Special Residential Homes for Confused Old People*, London, Longman.
2. Figures from the Department of Health 2002 indicated that 92 per cent of residential care homes were in the private or voluntary sector.
3. John Bayley wrote about his marriage to Iris Murdoch and her struggle with Alzheimer's disease in his books *Iris: A Memoir of Iris Murdoch*, London, Duckworth 1998 and *Iris and the Friends: A Year of Memories*, London, Duckworth 1999.
4. See for example Margaret Forster's autobiographical work *Precious Lives*, London, Chatto & Windus 1998 about the death of her father and her sister in law, her biographies in *Good Wives*, London, and her biographically based novel *Have the Men Had Enough?*
5. A. N. Wilson's recent biography, *Iris Murdoch As I Knew Her* London, Hutchinson 2003, paints a very different picture of Iris Murdoch.
6. Vonnegut, K. (1964) Tomorrow, tomorrow and tomorrow, in T. Boardman (ed.) *Connoisseur's Science Fiction*, Harmondsworth, Penguin

REFERENCES

Bytheway, B. (1993a) Ageing and biography: the letters of Bernard and Mary Berenson, *Sociology* 27(1): 153–165

Bytheway, B. (1993b) The ageing of Mary Berenson, in J. Johnson and R. Slater (eds) *Ageing and Later Life*, London, Sage.

Shields, C. (2003) Beautiful youth, *The Guardian: Review*, 26 July, p. 29.

Thompson, P., Itzin, C. and Abendstern, M. (1990) *I Don't Feel Old*, Oxford, Oxford University Press.

THE AUTHORS

Joanna Bornat, Professor of Oral History, School of Health and Social Welfare, the Open University.

Margaret Morganroth Gullette, Resident Scholar, Woman's Studies Research Centre, Brandeis University, MA, USA.

Mike Hepworth, Reader, Department of Sociology and Anthropology, University of Aberdeen.

Julia Johnson, Senior Lecturer, School of Health and Social Welfare, the Open University.

Jill Manthorpe, Professor of Social Work, Social Care Workforce Research Unit, King's College London.

Hannah Zeilig, freelance researcher on ageing issues.